MW00944685

THE OTHER SIDE OF ALZHEIMER'S

What Happens to You When
Your Spouse Has Alzheimer's

A Collection of Personal Experiences by a Woman Who Lived
Through Ten Years of Her Husband's Alzheimer's

Martha-Lee B. Ellis

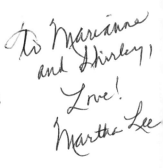

BALBOA.
PRESS

A DIVISION OF HAY HOUSE

Balboa Press books may be ordered through booksellers or by contacting:

Balboa Press
A Division of Hay House
1663 Liberty Drive
Bloomington, IN 47403
www.balboapress.com
1-(877) 407-4847

ISBN: 978-1-4525-4571-4 (sc)
ISBN: 978-1-4525-4570-7 (e)

Library of Congress Control Number: 2012900544

Because of the dynamic nature of the Internet, any web addresses or
links contained in this book may have changed since publication and
may no longer be valid. The views expressed in this work are solely those
of the author and do not necessarily reflect the views of the publisher,
and the publisher hereby disclaims any responsibility for them.

The author of this book does not dispense medical advice or prescribe the use
of any technique as a form of treatment for physical, emotional, or medical
problems without the advice of a physician, either directly or indirectly. The
intent of the author is only to offer information of a general nature to help
you in your quest for emotional and spiritual well-being. In the event you use
any of the information in this book for yourself, which is your constitutional
right, the author and the publisher assume no responsibility for your actions.

Printed in the United States of America

Balboa Press rev. date: 3/2/2012

IN MEMORY OF

Michael P.W. Ellis

my husband, who was lost to me through
Alzheimer's and was found again through these
words, with all the memories of a complete life
together.

DEDICATIONS

To Judith A. Shotts, former director of the Ruth Sheets Adult Care Center, Raleigh, NC; who walked every step of this journey with me with wisdom, compassion, strength and love . . .

To my son Matthew Gates Giovinetti, who traveled over 1,000 miles many times to provide caring support, respite and enduring love, all of which live in a special place in my heart which shall always be for him only . . .

To my family, whose support and love for both of us reached from near and far, and touched me always with gratitude.

SPECIAL THANKS

. . . to the Board of Directors and the staff of Frankie Lemmon School and Developmental Center, Raleigh, NC, whose generosity of understanding made it possible for me to continue as Director of the school during these years of living with Alzheimer's.

. . . to my writing instructor Alice Osborn and to my writers' group, who read, commented, corrected, laughed and cried with me, and gave me the courage to share these experiences.

. . . to Michelle Brovitz, freelance editor, for her excellence in copyediting this manuscript.

. . . to all the family members and caregivers, past and present, who contributed to my understanding of living with Alzheimer's disease through the Family Support Group for those of us with loved ones with Alzheimer's.

. . . to the staff and volunteers of the Ruth Sheets Adult Care Center, Raleigh, NC.

And finally, to Edenton Street United Methodist Church, Raleigh, NC, which ensures that the Ruth Sheets Adult

Care Center continues its mission to serve families and participants who benefit in numerous ways from the center's exemplary services of safety, care and dignity of life for frail older adults.

Letter from the Author

Dear Reader:

When your spouse has Alzheimer's disease, he or she is not the only one who changes. The other side of this disease is your side, reflected in how you change and how you feel about yourself as you do. Sometimes it is with growing understanding, and sometimes it is from desperation and even despair. Living with Alzheimer's exacts a huge toll on your mind, body and spirit, and you often wonder if you can survive it. You can, as I'm here to tell you.

When I began seeking information as soon as my husband was diagnosed, the information was often overwhelming. It made me doubt, in the fear and uncertainty of what was ahead for us, my ability to learn enough to care for him. I had no idea how to care for myself. Perhaps these chapters will give you a bit of insight into that part, which has to do with accepting yourself as you do the best you can.

I began writing about my own experiences, not as a guide but as a friend. I know of few other circumstances as hard to discuss with those who have not been there. Each chapter was written as a stand-alone article, so as not to discourage anyone who just needed to know that others feel the same things when facing each formidable task.

The experiences I share here focus on the effect of Alzheimer's on marriage, but the emotions are largely inclusive of all those involved in caring for any loved one with dementia.

My experiences, my decisions, my actions, were all my own. They do not have to be yours. They carry only the hope that some of them will connect with your experience in a way that gives you strength.

If you are, or know someone who is, living with someone who has Alzheimer's, we are friends. It's a large group, but narrowly defined by the experiences that only this disease introduces into your life.

Read this one page or one chapter at a time, as you feel the need. You are not alone. You are included in a select group of people who can and do survive living with Alzheimer's as well as the other, your, side of it. You have friends who have done it and who can and will understand your journey.

Blessings,
Martha-Lee Ellis

THE OTHER SIDE OF ALZHEIMER'S

What Happens to You When Your Spouse has Alzheimer's

A Collection of Personal Experiences by a Woman Who Lived Through Ten Years of Her Husband's Alzheimer's

★ A portion of this chapter was published in <u>Med Monthly</u> magazine, September/October 2011 issue: *www.medmonthly.com*

★★ A portion of this chapter was published by the title of "Who Are You?" in <u>Carolina Woman</u> magazine, August 2010 issue: *www.carolinawoman.com*.

Note: With two exceptions, all names other than Michael's and mine are pseudonyms. The names Judy Shotts, former director of the Ruth Sheets Adult Care Center, and Matt (Giovinetti), my son, are included with permission.

M-L. B. Ellis

CHAPTER ONE

JOURNEY INTO ALZHEIMER'S

Reactions before and after the diagnosis

One

Journey into Alzheimer's

As I approached the driveway of our home after work one afternoon, I was surprised to see my husband Michael's car already there, which was unusual. I walked in and saw him sitting in his wingback chair watching television. He said he felt fine, in answer to my question about his coming home early. I turned left, continuing on through the dining room, and was shocked to see the window broken. Glass was all over the floor.

"Michael!" Did you see this broken window?" I exclaimed, immediately thinking our house had been broken into.

"Yes. I broke it," he said, without getting out of his chair.

"What happened?" I asked, completely at a loss.

"I lost my house keys and had to get in somehow," was his almost off-hand reply, as though that should have been obvious to me. I stood there in stunned silence, not making sense of anything. My mind replayed coming through the front door and there had been nothing said about lost keys, not to mention a broken window. There had been no attempt to clean up the shards of glass or to tape something over the gaping window. To say that I thought this extremely strange is to put it mildly. It frightened me, to be honest. I asked again if he felt alright, thinking something must be very, very wrong. As I reflect back on it, something was, indeed, very wrong, but I just didn't know what it was. I asked him to help me clean up and tape over the window, which he was perfectly willing to do. I called someone to come and replace the glass and our evening went on as though nothing out of the ordinary had happened. At least, that's the way Michael's evening went. Mine was filled with feelings of discomfort, disbelief and distress.

Michael and I had experienced at least three years, probably more, of noticing his memory becoming increasingly worse, and now it seemed unlikely that it was just a normal process of aging forgetfulness. He was more than twenty years my senior and in his seventies, had a Ph.D. degree and owned a small engineering and manufacturing company. He was a gentleman, a well-rounded intellectual, and he had the best sense of humor

I had ever encountered. He was fun, and he was my best friend.

The broken window incident was followed not long after by two more inexplicable events. We were at the breakfast table one morning when he picked up a familiar box-shaped case with a simple snap closure containing an item he wanted. He began banging it on the side of the table, saying in frustration, "There must be a way to get into this damn thing!" I felt a frisson of fear race through me. How could he not know how to open it? Couldn't he see the snap on the flap?

The final occurrence which confirmed in my mind that we needed advice happened after dinner one evening. He was clearing away the dishes, which he did every bit as often as I did, and asked for directions for opening the dishwasher. *Opening the dishwasher?* Thinking I must not have heard him correctly, but looking at the closed but not locked dishwasher, I was tentative in opening it for him which would surely cause him to be embarrassed. I expected him to say with some exasperation, "Oh, yes, now I remember. Of course," but neither embarrassment nor exasperation happened. He thanked me for showing him how it opened, and the now familiar lump of fear lodged in my throat. Sleep eluded me that night. His forgetfulness had reached a state that I considered urgent, while he acted as if there were nothing strange at all about these incidents.

We agreed in the next few days that I would accompany Michael to see our internist physician, Dr. Smith, for his regular appointment the next week and talk about the memory problems. The physical examination went routinely well, and at the end Dr. Smith asked Michael if he had any questions.

"Doc, I can't remember a damn thing. Can you give me something to cure that?" Standing off to one side, I nodded emphatically at Michael's words. Dr. Smith asked us to explain, and Michael talked honestly about losing things and forgetting things.

I added my input: "Sometimes he forgets how things work. Once he couldn't remember how to open a snap closure on a box, or how to open the dishwasher."

Michael laughed a little and said, "See? I don't even remember those things!"

Dr. Smith smiled, started writing on his pad, and said, "I have a friend, a neurologist, who knows much more about this than I do. He specializes in memory problems, and I want you to see him. Here's his name and address."

As we sat in the neurologist's examination room two weeks later for Michael's appointment with Dr. Andrews, I picked up a copy of Reader's Digest and began reading aloud all the humorous excerpts I could find to alleviate our nervous anxiety. We laughed so much that I was concerned about disturbing people in other rooms. Dr. Andrews entered to find us smiling and chatting, and must have wondered if the reason we were there were serious at all.

After discussing our concerns with us, Dr. Andrews and his nurse put Michael through some simple motor movement exercises, asked him to repeat a few things in correct order, and to copy some geometric shapes with paper and pen. It seemed to me a straightforward basic glimpse at the way Michael processed information and directions. We left that appointment with recommendations for getting an MRI and a psycho-social evaluation, and instructions to return later for a consultation about the results. After these were scheduled and done over the next interminable weeks, we went back to Dr. Andrews for the final diagnosis. It was Alzheimer's-type dementia. I watched my husband's face crumple for a mere second or two as I myself struggled to breathe, and then Michael straightened his back and we walked out. He assured me all the way to the car that I needn't worry, because he wasn't about to let this thing beat him. I smiled weakly but was utterly terrified, my heart pounding and my thoughts not even coherent. Forty-five minutes had started to make a huge difference in our lives. I didn't know at the time just how life-changing this diagnosis would become, but my instincts were instantly in dread mode.

For the next two weeks or so, as I watched for Michael to come home from his office at the end of the day, it was as though I were expecting a stranger to walk through the door. Someone with a label across him like a banner, proclaiming his new identity as a person with Alzheimer's disease. Of course he was the same person who had walked out that door in the morning, which had the odd effect of being comforting and confusing at the same time.

I began to doubt that I had heard the doctor correctly. I tried to persuade myself that what I had really heard was that it was <u>not</u> Alzheimer's. I was going through my days in such a state of confusion that it was exhausting. I finally decided that I had to talk to the neurologist again, this time alone, and made the appointment. It was as the date approached that I had my first rational thought, realizing that I needed to have someone with me who would hear what I would hear, good or bad. I asked a nurse friend to accompany me, and we both heard the same thing: it was the bad news.

Michael and I were, without a chance of reversing course, on our journey into Alzheimer's, which is confusing, unrelenting, continuing sometimes slowly but steadily nonetheless. The course it follows is never clearly mapped with directions or signposts announcing where you are or how much farther you have to go. The road begins with unexpected curves and declines, then suddenly seems to go straight uphill into unknown territory. It forces a struggle to find your footing and enough stamina to search for some kind of level ground. Sometime later you feel that you are spiraling downhill too fast, with no time to catch your breath or to grab onto something that will steady you and slow the pace. It is a journey that relentlessly unfolds before you, out of your control. It is tacked onto years of countless sets of lost office and house and car keys, forgotten appointments both social and business, struggles with finding words in conversation, and oddly strange behaviors.

Ours was a journey of steep hills and shallow valleys, paths that wound up as blind alleys, bleak days and black nights. There were roads dimly lit at first, which would eventually, sometimes, become illuminated with understanding and acceptance. There were stops along the way in places of fear and heartbreak, grief, loneliness and loss; but there were also places of rare moments to savor and of touching love. It took seven more years to complete; more than ten years in all to reach the final destination, the journey finished.

It took another two years for me to realize that love is far more enduring than any disease; which, in the end, brought me to a peaceful place in my heart. I finally reached that level ground that had eluded us for so long. It was not the same place from which we started, but then it could not be. There had been too many twists and turns, too many challenges to climb over and too much time to traverse the distance.

The other side of Alzheimer's is yours, and it creates something within you that you could not have anticipated in different circumstances. It can strengthen or weaken, awaken commitment and love or despair and illness. With support and knowledge, you can find that your own journey is a revelation through which you discover a deeper understanding of life's challenges and blessings.

Surviving living with Alzheimer's is indeed possible, and your journey can end in peace. Give it time. It is love that matters; the love that was there at the beginning of your marriage. Go back to it, take the time to feel it and hold on to it. It may be difficult, shadowed as it is for much of the time, but it is there. It is love that brings the grace of peace. It is love that enables you to survive living with Alzheimer's.

CHAPTER TWO

PUZZLING PIECES

The confusion of learning how to live
when your spouse has Alzheimer's

Two

Puzzling Pieces

Life is a puzzle: a dynamic and fluid force, often requiring us to alter the expectations we have of the way things should be. We envision a picture and fit the pieces together to complete it, even when they have to be re-shaped and re-placed. Most of the time we manage to keep the image of the picture relatively intact. But nothing is more confusing than picking your way through the pieces of life created by your spouse having Alzheimer's disease. You are looking at the pieces of a new jigsaw puzzle spread everywhere around you, with every day a new puzzle.

When you live with Alzheimer's, there is no pretty picture on a box to show you how it should look or how to begin putting the pieces together. Some days have very little shape, no pleasing colors and pieces with sharp edges that actually hurt to touch. Some pieces are quite large, making them difficult to grasp, while others are small but critical to the picture. It is just human nature to try to create order when chaos enters your life, which is why we try to put the pieces of the Alzheimer's puzzle together. Searching for something that makes sense, that we can recognize, is a way of coping with things when our lives have, indeed, become scattered bits and pieces of a once-whole picture.

Many people have this puzzle and no two are exactly alike. How to begin making things fit together is an elusive, frustrating, lonely and exhausting process. Even if there were a set of directions, one set would not necessarily fit a different puzzle. There are, however, similarities in our responses to the challenges, many which mirror those of others'. There are some of the same things to learn, even as we work on the variations that are our own Alzheimer's puzzle.

Denial is the characteristic of major pieces, but they are still difficult to identify and link. Many times they get left in the scattered pile and never become part of the whole. My own experience with denial went on for a long time and exacted a painful price of frustration. I had no idea that acceptance of the stages of Alzheimer's, rather than denying them, would make working with them easier. It took being part of a support group of people who were also living with Alzheimer's to show me the truth and wisdom about that.

The pieces of fear are fairly outstanding. Fear creeps in when you finally realize that all your attempts to explain and correct behaviors are totally unsuccessful, which was certainly true in our case and in many others, I learned. Watching the same forgetfulness and mistakes after a while prompted me to give reminders often.

"Do you have your house keys?" "Do you need to put gas in your car?" "Remember that we have to be at the birthday dinner tonight by 7:00."

By far the most common tactic at this stage is to leave notes, mostly taping them to the front or back door. My favorite place was taping them to the dashboard of Michael's car. The notes would end up in his pocket or crumpled underfoot on the car floor, forgotten and unheeded. He still would forget the thing the note had been about. The reminders, verbal or written, inevitably become increasingly ineffective. Pieces of the Alzheimer's puzzle are everywhere you are.

One thing that seems to be common in many Alzheimer's cases is the phenomenon of forgetting how to do familiar tasks. We had already experienced Michael's not knowing how to open a simple snap closure on a box and not remembering how to open the dishwasher, and this type of memory loss continued. One day when we were engaged in a minor household repair, I saw Michael look with confusion at the screw I had handed him to replace a missing one.

"I think we need to use a screwdriver," I said tentatively, not understanding why he was hesitating.

"Do we have such a thing?" he asked. I hurried to the toolbox and returned with the screwdriver. When he didn't take it, I inserted the screw and began turning it with the screwdriver.

I stopped and asked, again tentatively, "Would you please finish it? You can tighten it much better than I can." He did, looking at the screwdriver with a big grin on his face when it was done.

"I've never seen anything like this in my life! It's a wonderful thing to have. Where did you find such a thing?" he inquired excitedly.

My breathing was shallow and rapid by then, and I had an acrid taste in my mouth as I answered around the lump in my throat, "I see these things in the store now and then." I walked away quickly, not wanting to look at him at that moment or have him see the emotions that must be showing on my face. It was disturbing and unreal, what should have been a normal moment in our lives, now broken into puzzling pieces.

One thing I did well, though, even after this and other similar incidents, was to continue going through my days as though life were still the picture I thought it should be. Not that that is a bad thing to do, but eventually it becomes impossible. The picture becomes blurred, the colors run and bleed, the outline faded and out of focus. The pieces don't fit together, and there is no pretty box to put them into, out of sight as far as denial makes that possible.

After Michael was enrolled in an adult day care center (see Chapter 6), he noticed how tired I was at the end of a long day when I collapsed on the sofa as soon as we got home. Even though I was surprised, it felt wonderful when he said, "What can I do for you to make you feel better?"

Knowing that fixing supper or taking me out to eat were not rational choices, I could think of nothing other than, "I would love a glass of water." He strode into the kitchen, and I heard cabinets and the pantry door open and close several times.

He came back into the living room and said, "And where would I find it?" I got up from the sofa and went with him into the kitchen, picked up a glass from the cabinet, turned on the water and filled the glass. Then, not knowing what else to do or what to say, I handed him the glass and returned to my seat on the sofa.

He came right behind me, proudly handed me the glass of water and said, "Let me know if there is anything else you need." What a painfully sweet thing had just happened. That piece of the puzzle had a jagged edge that hurt, even with the sweet form. It was one of those pieces I didn't know where to put; it didn't seem to fit anywhere. That was the end of my days that were crafted from denial. The Alzheimer's picture was now clearer than the picture of our life as it should have been.

The pain that becomes a constant companion to the beating of your heart and the breaths you draw is so much a part of you that you reach a point where you don't remember not having it. I honestly could not let myself think of how our marriage used to be, because that magnified the hurt and was almost unbearable. The only way to get through the days was to live each moment at a time.

Although Michael had continued taking showers without assistance, I heard him yell one morning when he stepped into it. I knew immediately that the water was scalding hot and that he no longer remembered how to adjust the temperature. I never let him take another shower that I didn't turn on the water for him. Not many days after the hot water incident, I noticed when he came out of the bathroom that he had not washed his hair. The next morning as he was getting in the shower, I said, "Remember to use the shampoo."

"What's that?" he asked.

Every day from then on, I would take his hand after he stepped in the shower, pour shampoo in it and say, "Rub it on your head like this . . ." Each time there was a loss of awareness or ability, the sadness inside me burrowed deeper into my heart.

There were many times during those years when I would notice the first time Michael didn't seem to know how to do something. I would sink into the depression of believing that another skill was gone, only to see him able to do it the next day and maybe for a while afterward. Eventually it would become apparent that that skill was, indeed, lost; but I could be grateful for the way it had slipped away gradually. I used to say that Heaven had given me a preview of what was going to happen later, rather than jar my heart with a sudden loss.

Life when you live with Alzheimer's is the epitome of confusion. There are times, however, when the puzzle pieces come marked for easy placement to make at least part of the picture recognizable. When Michael would call me by name after not doing so for weeks; when he remembered meaningful things about our family; when he told me he had to return to the Air Force after watching the events of September 11 on television: these were the things that made him who he was. These were the pieces that fit together with love and comfort.

Other parts of our life picture would sometimes appear, too, adding the sound of levity to the shape and form of one of our days. These were the pieces that made a beautiful scene. When Michael used the electric leaf blower that had a habit of coming loose where the plug joined the handle, he would yell each time it quit, "This damn thing's out of gas!" I learned quickly to stay nearby, since I would need to walk to where he was, plug it back in, and leave him for the next two minutes or so (if I were lucky) and he'd have a happy afternoon doing what he loved to do. I would also invariably end up laughing at the spectacle we made of ourselves in the back yard. Humor was far more important than Alzheimer's disease and any puzzling phase of life.

The times when we shared laughter were special. When we laughed, we laughed together and it was a bond that kept the memory alive of how important and meaningful laughter had been before and during our marriage. It was a wonderful feeling, like going back to a beloved home after being away too long. I still love gazing at that picture in my mind, alive with the sound of shared moments.

While you are living with Alzheimer's, you cannot stop trying to put your life together, no matter how many pieces have broken and become scattered. It was not possible for me to put together the whole Alzheimer's jigsaw puzzle during the more than ten years we lived through it. Perhaps, after all, that was not necessary. Maybe some pieces were not meant to fit with other pieces after time, and maybe some pieces were better off left to the side and not all that important. It might well be that losing some pieces altogether was insignificant. The final picture for every person ends up being different from the image we tried so hard to create when we first looked at the puzzle of life with Alzheimer's.

With patience and love, however, you can find enough pieces to make some parts of the picture whole, which are the pieces that fit the heart of your life together. Place them gently within the framework of the strength you discover in yourself as you survive living with Alzheimer's, understanding with clarity the words, ". . . and the greatest of these is love."

(1 Corinthians 13:13)

MARRIAGE: MEMORIES THAT MATTER

Issues of marriage that affect you in dealing with Alzheimer's

Three

Marriage: Memories that Matter

Taking a step back from the mirror that hung above my long, low dresser, I knew I was looking at myself with surprise as I put down my Heavenly Pink lipstick. Not at the way I had fixed my hair or the colors I had chosen carefully to wear, but at the thoughts I had just had. It was New Year's Eve and I was getting ready to go out for an early dinner with Michael, whom I had been dating for six years. My first husband's death had been nine years before and I had steadfastly refused Michael's several proposals of marriage for the last three, mostly because of obstacles that existed only in my head. My thoughts at the moment had startled me. I heard myself thinking, *I could probably spend the rest of my life getting dressed to go out with Michael, waiting for him to arrive, and telling him good night as he left later.* It was not a smug thought even though it could easily have been interpreted as such had I spoken it aloud. No, it actually was accompanied with a feeling of emptiness . . . maybe more correctly a sense of being incomplete.

Michael was almost 25 years older than I and his children were grown and on their own. My son was thirteen years old. Two things always came into play when Michael suggested marriage: it just didn't seem fair for him to take on rearing another teenager when he had already gone through that with four of his own; and, I didn't think I could go through the death of my husband another time. Given our age difference, the odds were that I would live longer than Michael. He had also been widowed many years earlier and I didn't want either of us to suffer that kind of loss again. Surprisingly, here I was, standing in front of the mirror wishing that I could marry this man, fully aware that I loved him more than I ever thought would be possible for me again. I knew with certainty that I always would, whether we married or not.

My first marriage, to a young man named Nicky, had lasted seven years. We had our son Matt, and four years later Nicky died in a fatal boating accident. It was now nine years later, and this New Year's Eve was prompting these unexpected thoughts.

During dinner that night Michael said rather casually, "Don't you want to get married before your birthday in June?"

I put down my salad fork, looked at him for a moment and answered, "Yes."

Just that night, while getting dressed, I had put to rest the fear of his dying before me, finally realizing that I could not go on living life being afraid of death. And I remembered his saying to me one time months before, when I told him I didn't want him to have to rear another young teenager, "That's not your decision to make. If I want to be part of Matt's life, it's my decision. I would welcome it."

This was a huge moment on that Eve, finally accepting the opportunity that he offered me again to become complete in the circle of love that enfolded us.

After hearing my "Yes," Michael leaned back in his chair, grinned, said, "Well, then, what date would suit you?" and proceeded to signal the waitress. Two glasses of champagne later there was a warm feeling surging through me that had nothing to do with wine. There was no feeling of surprise, either. Just that feeling of "all's right with the world."

We had a beautiful evening wedding in my living room at the end of May, with my family and his children, including his two grandchildren, as delighted witnesses. It was hard to tell who was more excited and happy, my son Matt or I.

When Michael kissed me chastely at the end of the ceremony, his son called out, "Oh, come on, Dad. You can do better than that!" So Michael proceeded to tip me back over his arm and laid a kiss on me that was meant to thrill the cream-colored shoes right off my feet.

My sisters and my mother had cooked and baked wonderful heavy hors d'oeuvres as well as the at-home wedding cake, and it was a festive scene in my townhouse. Michael and I had made reservations for the night at the hotel where we were to receive our friends for a large reception the next afternoon. My mother, noticing that I didn't eat anything except the ritual wedding cake bite after the ceremony, asked me quietly if I wanted her to fix a container of food for us to take to the hotel. I gratefully agreed, and she and my sisters packed up food enough to serve the reception the next day. When we were leaving, jokes, laughter, ribald suggestions (from his children, not my family, you understand), and general hilarity ushered us out the door. At the hotel's bridal suite, we discovered that our family members had delivered flowers and a bottle of liqueur for our first night, and it was then that I realized I had walked out the door at home without the food Mother had thoughtfully packed for us. It didn't seem to matter, though.

The reception the next day was large, fun and truly special. The formal wedding cake was gorgeous, the food was phenomenal, and the guests were in high good humor.

My mother, knowing that I was too excited to eat, instructed the wait staff to fix two containers of food for us to take with us on our trip. Again, when it was time to leave, the high good humor reached a fever pitch that accompanied us out the door. Rice cascaded over us and into the car, which was the only food that left the reception with us.

An hour or so later, driving down the highway, Michael looked at me and said, "Do you think I need to lose weight?" I looked at him with surprise, and he continued, "I just say that because I noticed that you never seem to take any food your mother goes to so much trouble to fix for us . . ." With a sly grin, he wheeled into the next fast food place we saw. The hamburgers and fries were delicious.

With that as a beginning, our marriage was off on its own path of high good humor. My life had indeed become complete again. We were quite financially well off though not actually wealthy, and loved doing things together with my son and various combinations of Michael's children and their families. I felt secure for the first time since I had been widowed almost ten years before.

Back home from our wedding trip, there was no question that Matt felt good about my new marriage. He answered the phone one evening during supper and I heard him say, "Wait a minute, I have to ask my mom and dad." Holding his hand over the speaker end of the phone, he leaned around where he could see us and whispered, "I love saying that . . . ask my mom and dad." He was a very content 14-year old who finally had a dad again to add to asking his mom for permission to do something.

Five years seemed to drift by, and my description of them could read like poetry. Probably the only surprises I encountered were the growing enjoyment of Michael's brilliant sense of humor and his gentle treatment and acceptance of Matt. He was one of those rare stepfathers who absolutely never interfered with my discipline of my son; never even offering a suggestion or correction of my parental decisions unless I asked him for it. He was then totally honest with me but never criticized me if he disagreed. I admired and respected him for that, and still do to this day.

Even poetic fairy-tales sometimes have endings other than "happily ever after." Our marriage began moving in one of those different directions about five years after the sublime beginning. Michael would turn away from any discussion I tried to have about how we were going to make our senior years financially secure. He was already in his sixties and still running the small engineering company he had formed. I explained several times that if anything ever happened to him, I wouldn't have any idea what I needed to do about his company or anything else.

When I asked one time if he had a will, he replied, "I've written down everything you need to know, so don't keep harping on it."

He was rude. Not abusive, but rude is not comforting. He pushed me aside emotionally, and I suffered from lack of sharing the "for richer or poorer" part of our vows. I felt disenfranchised, as though our marriage partnership was far less a partnership than I had always thought. His responses made me feel as though he thought I only had a selfish interest in my own comfort, with no regard for the comfort of our family. His closed and abrupt attitude puzzled me greatly. I was hurt and angry, and completely unable to bridge the gap. That never changed.

I stopped asking or mentioning it for a long time, but it always lingered with me that I truly wouldn't know what to do if he should become incapacitated or, heaven forbid, die.

Once during this unsettled time, I met him at his bookkeeper's office to sign our income tax forms. She said, not altogether jokingly, "Mike, when are you going to let go of this business that's just costing you money and have some fun going fishing?"

That night I said, "I think it's time for you to tell me what's going on with the company." Blunt. Right to his face. He said nothing. So I continued, asking if the company were doing well and finally realizing the answer

I feared. He simply told me not to worry, as usual, which increased my need to know about our financial security.

I continued talking, until he said abruptly, "I don't need to talk about this. Everything's fine."

Getting more frustrated, I countered with, "So, we'll be able to retire and live comfortably ever after? What happens if you die? Will the company have debts?" No answer. "Are your children going to expect an inheritance from you?"

Then, in a statement that chilled me, he answered, "My children think I have plenty of money, and they aren't going to be told anything else."

Staring at him, I asked, "So you're going to leave it for me to tell them there's nothing there?"

"Yes," he said. "Better you than me," and walked away. I was hurt beyond measure, picturing that my good relationship with his children would be damaged, not to mention the potential legal issues he might be setting up for me to handle.

Although this in and of itself might not seem such a major problem, there were situations and contingencies surrounding his company and his solvency that kept becoming apparent to me. I could not persuade him to explain anything to me that involved money. In a rare conversation once years before, he had told me he was putting what he considered my household allowance into a savings account toward the purchase of a new house. Now, when I asked him about that, he told me matter-of-factly that since it was his money, he had used it for the company. It was all gone.

A couple of years later, he developed a very painful hip deterioration condition and eventually needed replacement surgery. Anesthesia left him with a paralyzed intestinal system, and the drug they administered to correct it caused him to have a psychotic reaction. He became violent and hallucinatory for three days. It took four of us to keep him under any semblance of control one entire night, which still lives as a huge nightmare in my memory. He was never the same again. As a matter of fact, his memories of hospitalization always were of the hallucinations he experienced rather than anything that had been real. Three years after that, he was diagnosed with the early stage of Alzheimer's disease. His neurologist told me later that indeed, if Alzheimer's were incipient at the time of surgery, his psychotic reaction to the drug was the same as an insult to the brain and could have caused the Alzheimer's to become active. If medical science were to dispute this possibility, I must bow to another explanation. I was emotionally wrought and should not be considered an expert in the development of his disease process. It is what I remember hearing, whether or not with accuracy.

Needless to say, I became more and more acutely worried about him, our life, our future, and the reality of our lack of finances. I told Michael that I was uncomfortable that neither of us had a will and that I was going to consult an attorney. I asked if he wanted to go with me. He opted not to, so I sat down and asked him to tell me how he wanted his will to read, with instructions about the company and the family. I made copious notes to take with me.

In the attorney's comfortable office the following week, I explained that Michael had become forgetful at times though he was still working; and what the accountant had said about the company and other details about our joint property. I gave him the notes I had prepared expressing Michael's wishes. Wills for each of us were prepared and mailed to us.

The attorney had instructed me to go over Michael's with him carefully to make sure he understood everything before we came to sign them and have them witnessed and filed. Michael did not disagree with anything on any page that we read together.

The day to sign our wills came, and as soon as we sat down with the attorney, Michael placed the copy of his will in front of the attorney and said, "I won't sign this. It's a piece of damn garbage."

I was speechless. He then proceeded to accuse the attorney of trying to make something very complicated out of something simple. He kept saying, "It doesn't take this many damn pages to say that I want her (gesturing to me) to have everything unless she dies first. You're just trying to get money that you don't deserve."

Embarrassment and incredulity filled every bone and sinew in my body and I turned on Michael, making a dreadful scene even worse. I hotly demanded to know why he had not told me that when we reviewed the will together, coming closer to throwing a full-blown temper tantrum than ever in my life, including childhood.

The attorney was more than wonderful, staying calm and listening. He finally said, "Let me re-do this; I think I know what you want."

I did not say one word on the way home that day, too distressed and angry to trust myself. I fixed some kind of lame supper and put it on a tray in front of the television, telling myself Michael was very lucky I didn't dump it in his lap. We said nothing other than necessary words during the entire evening.

Two days later we received in the mail a revised, shorter will. I didn't even read it with Michael, but I called and made another appointment for us with the attorney. I told him that I would come with Michael, but I would remain in the lobby and not join them for their discussion of his will. I knew the attorney would need to be very sure that Michael understood and agreed with the shorter version and that I should not sit in with them. Somehow, I knew Michael might feel that he had to put on a show of knowledge for my benefit, and that was pointless. If the attorney had any doubts about Michael's ability to comprehend, so be it. This had to be done without me.

Sitting in the lobby while Michael met with the attorney was excruciatingly nerve-wracking. Eventually I heard the attorney invite other people in to witness the will, and even heard laughter. When they all came out, everyone was smiling and the attorney nodded significantly to me. It was done. I would know what to do at the time of Michael's death, whenever that might occur in the future.

In my opinion, there has never existed a single problem that stayed neatly tied together without extending to other situations and circumstances, and our financial battle certainly had far-reaching fingers. It touched many parts of our lives not even concerned with money. It colored my feelings and our relationship. It dampened our passion and cast a pallid gloom over my marriage experience, even though it never seemed to touch Michael. For him, the only problem about money was me. He had never worried about financial security. He quite simply believed that however reduced our circumstances were, he would always be able to fix it. He was a dreamer, and his dreams had nothing but happy endings. But his dream of wealth dwindled away and never materialized again in our life together.

Michael drifted away from me further and further as time went by and Alzheimer's claimed more and more of his mental acuity. There came a time when I could not carry sadness over our marriage and sadness about him at the same time. It would not be possible to survive such pain. I knew that I would never hear him explain or apologize for making me suffer the uncertainties of financial ruin, but I had to let go of the marital problems. I had to care only about the man I had loved and stay by him as Alzheimer's relentlessly changed him. My sadness became one of losing my companion, my friend, my happiness, my life and my husband. And, too, solving the problems of keeping him safe and giving him whatever he needed to remain with me as long as he could were almost overwhelming in their complexity.

The message here is, I know, that no matter what unresolved issues may be in your life when Alzheimer's claims your spouse, you can only survive living through it if you let the problems go. You will face trials much more significant than bank accounts or disrespectful behaviors or whatever may have been part of your married life. You will face life with a spouse who is no longer capable of solving problems or understanding simple things, and eventually life with a spouse who doesn't even know who you are. Too many things have to do with health, safety and end-of-life issues. You will have to make decisions alone, for the most part. If you were able earlier to make health-care and end-of-life decisions together, you will have to carry them out alone. Don't hang on to past issues that belonged to the two of you. They belong to you only, eventually. Your life through Alzheimer's is heavy enough without dragging the past along, too.

In time, you will be grateful if you are fully present with the circumstances that Alzheimer's disease brings to you. Forgiveness and love are the foundations of peace and the strength of surviving. It takes effort, but they are there if you look for them.

In the end, you will have survived your marriage and your side of Alzheimer's. You deserve to feel the grace of peace and to survive living with Alzheimer's, too.

DRIVING THE DECISION

When to stop your spouse from driving

Four

Driving the Decision

Charmed lives, guardian angels, Divine intervention, or plain good luck: choose one or all, something prevented catastrophe when it came to the issue of restricting Michael's driving.

In the early days, after the diagnosis of his Alzheimer's disease, it was sometimes easy just to go along pretty much as always, albeit with a sense of caution and heightened awareness. If I were to be completely honest, I would have to say that many decisions which had to be made were not necessarily driven by proper planning. After all, how do you plan for something that hasn't happened yet? It's a hard lesson to learn, and we were fortunate that our experience with Michael's driving did not result in physical injury to anyone. The emotional injury to me was almost as serious and talking about it might help someone else do better with preventive measures than I did.

From the very day we were given the diagnosis, my mind raced ahead to the what-ifs, the what-whens, and the what-will-we-do thoughts. But that's not the time of reality. That's the time when you are confused and cannot peer into the future far enough to understand exactly what you are facing. You are holding on as tightly as possible to the *now*—the "we're still fine" time. Planning ahead is not possible then, or wasn't for me, because I didn't know what, when or how to anticipate the impact of the events that Alzheimer's brings with it.

As time progressed through weeks and a few months, with nothing changing very drastically, we tended to fall into a place where Alzheimer's was more a word than something that changed our lives. Change did come, inevitably, sometimes creeping up on us and sometimes with sudden drama.

Michael was still driving to work daily, and there was no reason to think he could not continue to do so for a while. Just to be sure, acknowledging the warnings from the literature and discussions with others about Alzheimer's, I rode in the car with him a couple of times a week. Most of the time this was going to his office with him on weekend days, a forty-five minute drive from home, camouflaging my intentions by asking that we make time to have lunch together. I never saw him speed, miss a stop-light, or drive in any way that would signal less than acute awareness of driving conditions. The problems arose, I discovered, when his routine routes were altered in any way.

The day came when I was expecting him back from a trip to the Outer Banks, familiar to him for more years than we had been married, and he called about the time he should have arrived home.

"I don't know where the hell I am," he said, "so I don't know what time I'll get home." This was from a bag-type car phone that you could carry with you, for which I was immediately grateful, even though I had not been pleased when he bought it.

"Do you see a parking lot where there are stores?" I asked, while desperately searching my mind for any idea at all.

"Yes, I see an Eckerd's over there," he answered.

"Well," I said, "drive on over there and take your phone into Eckerd's and ask for the manager. Tell the manager that your wife wants to speak to him." I heard him hang up and after several fraught minutes, he called and told me the manager was with him and would speak to me.

"Hi, my name is Martha, and this man is my husband. His name is Mike, and he seems to have gotten off his familiar route to Raleigh. Where are you located?" I asked.

"Oh, we're in the Oak Shopping Center, ma'am." He sounded like a teenager who might have just started driving himself.

My query following this information would have been embarrassing had I not been very frightened: "I really need to know what town you're in," I said in a voice much brighter than I felt.

"Why, this is Goldsboro, ma'am," he answered, registering a little note of surprise in his voice.

I immediately felt extremely helpless and a bit desperate. How was I going to get Michael home again? "Do you know how to get to US 70 from there, and is it far?" I asked, trying to sound confident and not scared.

"Oh, it's simple from here, ma'am," he responded.

"Would you be so kind as to write down the directions for my husband?" I asked, in what I hoped was an unconcerned tone. Assuring me he would be glad to do that, and after I asked to speak to Michael again, the young manager handed him the phone.

"Michael, this nice young man is going to write down directions for you. When you get back in the car, call me and read them to me so we can get you to US 70

44

together." Minutes passed, more than could possibly have been necessary, and my panic increased with every breath I drew.

Finally, I dialed his car number. "Have you found the way to US 70 yet?"

"Hell, no. That guy didn't have any idea of the right way to go," was the dreaded response.

"Do you see a street sign where you are?" I prompted.

He answered, "No, but there is probably one at the next corner."

Thank goodness. I needed an intersection for the plan that had formed in my mind. My voice was quiet and confident as I said, "Don't hang up. I want you to drive just up to that corner and park. Read the street sign to me and also tell me the name of the street that turns off there." I was terrified that he would become exasperated and frustrated by this time and perhaps just drive on, no telling where, but he willingly complied with my suggestion.

"This street is Elm," he said, "and the one that turns is Oak."

"That is perfect, Michael. I want you to stay right there, don't go anywhere else, and I'm going to send someone to help you get to US 70. Just stay parked right there."

Realizing for the last several minutes, which seemed like hours, that I could not possibly get to Goldsboro from Raleigh before he would forget that I was coming, or find him if I got there, I knew I had to call the Goldsboro police. The voice that answered the phone was a kind and mature voice, a man who never indicated alarm or impatience during our entire conversation.

I told him my name and said, "My husband has somehow gotten off US 70 to Raleigh and cannot find his way back to it."

"Does he have a car phone, ma'am?"

"Yes, he does, and I have told him to park at the intersection of Elm and Oak Streets."

"Give me the phone number, Mrs. Ellis, and I'll call him and give him directions."

With a sinking heart but somehow managing a normal voice (from where that came I'll never know), I replied "I don't think he'll be able to follow directions. He may get confused since he's in a strange location." I couldn't breathe at that point, being sure that this kind law enforcement officer would all of a sudden feel he needed to protect the Goldsboro citizenry and the motoring public in general, and send someone to haul Michael into jail. Well, at least I'd have time to get there without Michael driving off into an unknown sunset . . .

"As it happens, Mrs. Ellis, we have an officer in that vicinity now, and I'll send him to lead Mr. Ellis out to 70." I don't know how my heart was still beating, but it was and I managed to describe Michael's car and stammer my profound gratitude. I called Michael immediately and asked if he were still parked at Elm and Oak.

"Well, yes, you told me to stay here. Uh oh, I've got to move on . . . a policeman is coming."

"WAIT, Michael, don't leave. He is coming to show you how to get back on the highway to come home." Panic like I've never felt before assailed my whole being.

Since Michael didn't hang up the phone, I heard a man's voice say, "Mr. Ellis, follow me, sir, and I'll lead you to US 70."

Michael picked up the phone, said "I'm leaving now," and I just said, "Call me when you're back on the highway," and hung up.

The state of disbelief, panic and terror I was in is indescribable. I thought if he ever got home, I'd never let him get behind the wheel of a car again. Never. The minutes ticked on with no phone call. Even as hesitant as I was to have him answer his phone while driving (after dark, now, of course), I called him. His answering voice was jovial and he announced that he had just seen a sign with a large number 70 on it, when I asked where he was.

I hastened to remind him that that 70 did not mean the speed limit and he was not to drive over 60 mph; the 70 was the highway number, which meant he was on the right road to get home.

The remaining hour was interminable as I waited to see his headlights turn into the driveway. I forced myself not to call his car phone again, which ranks up there with the highest degree of self-restraint ever exhibited by a human being, I'm sure. When those headlights illuminated our front window, I dashed out to greet him getting out of the car. Masking my near-hysteria, I hugged him and told him how glad I was it had all worked out. I babbled on about how helpful the police had been and how kind they were to find him and lead him to the highway.

The end of this drama was still more of a drama. Michael looked at me after I finished gushing over him and about the Goldsboro police, and he denied all of it. He made me understand in no uncertain terms, speaking to me with anger and clearly indicating that I was making up a fantastic story, that there had never been any police. The only reason he was late was the fault of a gas station attendant who sent him in the wrong direction. To this day, I do not know if Michael didn't remember this entire saga once he got home, or if he simply denied it so I wouldn't worry. It was abundantly clear to me, though, that I needed to be careful in the future about relating details to him that might suggest he had needed to be rescued in any way. My heart still flutters with the memory of panic when I recall this traumatic event, even though it became traumatic only for me. Michael never mentioned it again. Nor was there any point in my doing so, because to him, it didn't happen.

The decision for him not to drive again was not far in the future, and came with another set of circumstances that did, in fact, prove to be the right choice. It was time to stop trusting in luck.

"Mom, it's been a while since I've been able to come home and give you a chance to get away for a couple of days," was the welcome greeting from my son Matt, calling from his home in Minneapolis. "I want you to accept the invitation to go with your girlfriends to the beach. You need a break and I have a break in my schedule. I'm coming, so you plan to go." Matt had come more often than I had any right to expect, but it had been a couple of months since he had last come to stay with Michael. Going to a South Carolina beach was like a dream. I hadn't been more than two or three hours from Michael since he showed progressive signs of Alzheimer's.

Matt and I decided that one way to entertain him while I was gone would be to go to Michael's sister's home in Wilmington, about two hours from our home in Raleigh. Another sister lived around the corner from her. The plan in place, I drove to South Carolina to meet my friends at the beach the day after Matt arrived, the same day they were leaving for Wilmington.

One night passed and the next morning I had a call from Matt. "Mom, I need to tell you a couple of things. One is that Mike would not let me drive the car to Wilmington. I had to tell him every time we were coming up on a car ahead too fast, and to slow down for the next curve. It was awful, but thank goodness he did what I told him to do. We got here OK, but my nerves are shot. He should not drive any more, Mom, and I'm going to disable his car. The other thing is that he won't stay in the house. He keeps saying he's going out to look for you, so we have to watch him constantly and go with him when he walks out the door." Going out to look for me meant standing along a busy thoroughfare. He was obviously confused, not being in his own home. He still knew who I was at that time and was searching for the only thing that would make him feel safe in a strange place.

"O K, son, I'm packing as we speak. Do what you have to do to disable the car. Let me speak to Michael so I can tell him I'll be there in a few hours." I did and started out, saying a distracted farewell to my friends. The beach was totally irrelevant, an already forgotten respite.

When I finally turned onto the residential street where his two sisters lived, I saw a group of people standing on the corner of the highway and the street. Matt, Michael, both of his sisters, and a friend of theirs were gathered together, shifting around and kicking up the dust in the hot July sun. I pulled over, got out and hugged Michael. When we were in the house, Michael proceeded to tell me that someone had stolen a part from his car and it wouldn't start. His sister had called the police (keeping her finger on the hook to stay disconnected), but they hadn't come yet. We pretended yet again to call a mechanic and I told Michael that I had been informed that the part to fix the car had to be ordered from a place in the far-west. We would have to go back to Raleigh and wait for his car to be fixed.

Michael never saw his car again and never drove again. He remembered that car far longer than he remembered anything else though, being angry and upset for weeks. He expected every day to be called to come get his car, and his anger only increased. All the literature and advice about persons with Alzheimer's and driving clearly states that the spouse or close family member should never be the one to take driving privileges away. The anger, such as Michael felt, most often turns into the "damn the messenger" syndrome and causes a great deal of conflict.

During those weeks, he had a routine appointment scheduled with his internist physician, and I sent Dr. Smith a message beforehand. I asked him to tell Michael he couldn't drive anymore, explaining what had happened and that Michael anticipated his car being returned. Dr.

Smith was wonderful. He told Michael that his blood pressure medicine had to be changed, and that he didn't allow patients taking this new medicine to drive. I did not have to be the one to tell Michael he couldn't drive. I was grateful beyond measure to Dr. Smith, although Michael had a far different opinion. When we left the appointment, Michael said sternly to me, "If that S-O-B thinks he's taking my driver's license away, he's got another think coming!" I kept quiet.

Months passed, and so did, finally, Michael's suspicion and anger about his car. In subsequent years, though, he would occasionally tell people that he had had three cars stolen and that none of them had ever been found. Why three, I can't explain but explanations were not necessary by then. It was the end of an uncomfortable, not to say fearful, phase in our lives. Michael himself had driven the decision that prevented him from driving.

This series of events figures, without question, as among the most difficult lessons I had to learn in living with Alzheimer's. I am filled with gratitude as I relate it for charmed lives, guardian angels, Divine intervention, good luck, or all. Surviving the challenges of Alzheimer's has to be more, sometimes, than making the right decisions. We were blessed.

Chapter Five

REFLECTIONS

*How you feel about yourself as you change
while living with Alzheimer's*

Five

Reflections

The bathroom mirror was slightly steamy, small rivulets of moisture moving slowly from top to bottom. My face, a little left of center, looked wavy and out of focus, reflecting the way I felt. I thought it was possible that my image would look the same in a perfectly clear mirror, because I was having more and more trouble recognizing myself all the time.

When your spouse has Alzheimer's disease, he or she is not the only one whose face in the mirror reflects someone who is changing. My husband Michael had the disease, but I began a process of changes that were every bit as significant as his; sometimes disturbing, often depressing, sometimes maturing, but constantly changing.

The obvious side of Alzheimer's was the one affecting Michael and was the result of the changes in the brain which altered his perceptions, emotions and behaviors. The other side affected me as a result of witnessing and experiencing those changes and caused a corresponding set of altered perceptions, emotions and behaviors. We responded to the awareness of his loss of understanding quite similarly for a while, each of us reacting with our own explanations and denials. Eventually his awareness faded, but mine only became sharper as I watched him become someone completely different from the person I had married. The mirror of our life began to crack.

I remember clearly how I tried to combat his memory lapses with careful explanations of the way things really had happened, the people who were really involved, the place and time events really had occurred. It was wasted effort, my denial that a disease was in play here and that I could not affect a cure. On some level, my reasoning was that if I could correct his memory of things, the disease would be kept at bay and he would be normal again. But what I saw was that my correcting made him uncomfortable, agitated and angry with me. I was not aware then that *I* needed to change. I was slow to learn that people with Alzheimer's are always right. No exceptions. There is never an explanation that can change their way of thinking or remembering something in a certain way.

Michael's effective way of proving he was right was by shaking his finger in my face and cursing at me. "Don't you try to tell me something different. I know what I'm talking about and it's none of your damn business, anyway," was a familiar retort that backed me right down into silence. I really hated that . . . it made me feel belittled and resentful when I was only trying to help, translated "correct." I was intimidated by his uncharacteristic defiance.

The resentment, uselessness and fear that I felt were very real ways in which I was a victim of Alzheimer's. It was an unanticipated side of the disease. I was the one who could think clearly and reasonably, but that turned out to be faint praise at best. It took me far too long to let go of the need to correct him and face the reality that being combative was unnecessary and unwise. The choice was to react or respond. Reacting only escalated our emotions into a cloudy, murky, unrecognizable version of our relationship. When I learned to respond with a smile and "Isn't that interesting" or something equally banal, at least our relationship retained a calm, although thin, veneer.

While Michael's behaviors indicated that everything he thought, said and did were absolutely right, my own behaviors became increasingly foreign to me. The battle I faced with myself about lying to him was one that haunted me day and night for most of the ten-plus years we lived through Alzheimer's. I lied to him. I hid things from him, denied things and sneaked around. All the things you associate with being untrustworthy and disloyal were suddenly the way I was conducting myself. I could not reconcile it with the person I thought I was. I had just hidden the mail before he could get to it, and it didn't matter that it was because I had found unpaid bills forgotten and stuffed between chair cushions. I put money from a joint account into a single one in my name, and it didn't matter that it was because I had found a statement that showed all of our savings gone for no apparent reason. I opened a new joint account with limited funds and sneaked the new checks into his usual checkbook holder and hid the former ones. It was much later when the disease had progressed even further that I asked my son to disable Michael's car so that he couldn't drive anymore. I pretended to call a mechanic and told Michael the necessary part had to be ordered from somewhere far away. The lies continued.

We had had the diagnosis of Alzheimer's for several months, although Michael was still driving to work every day at this time. I had been with him in his accountant's office recently when she had remarked that he ought to close up his business and "go fishing," instead of running a company that was only costing him money. I had begun paying attention to our finances then, and that had prompted the things I did that made me feel so uncomfortable.

Finally realizing that I needed a Power of Attorney to protect our finances, I had one prepared. The problem with that was that Michael's current stage of Alzheimer's made him question with suspicion any suggestion or activity that was the slightest bit unusual. Would he ever assign his power of attorney to me? I seriously doubted it and spent anxious days trying to find a solution.

Deciding I needed another opinion, I called his business accountant, Sharon, and asked if she thought I needed Michael's power of attorney. "Of course you do," she replied. "I've been worried for some time that you didn't have it. I've mentioned it to Mike but he doesn't think it's necessary. You're both going to end up with nothing if you don't take control."

With my heart pounding and heavy as I listened to her, I said, "I've had one drawn up, but I don't know how I'll persuade him to sign it."

"He's coming in for his monthly appointment next Monday at 11:00. If you come and bring the Power of Attorney with you, I'll take care of the persuading, we'll have it witnessed, and I'll notarize it." She was confident and assured. I wasn't, but I knew it was probably my best chance. Michael had worked with Sharon for many years and trusted her implicitly.

When Monday morning arrived, I said to Michael as we were getting dressed, "I know you mentioned seeing Sharon today at 11:00. I think I'll come and we can talk with her about your retiring, sooner or later. She might have some advice." I was counting on his not remembering whether he had told me about meeting with her. He didn't, but he didn't comment on my suggestion, either.

Somehow, I knew he wouldn't trust me; or in my guilt-ridden and lying heart, I supposed he wouldn't. I was right. But then, I didn't trust him, either, to accept my being with him to talk to Sharon. I was right again.

I let him start out fifteen minutes before me, which was about 7:30 a.m., then drove the forty-five minutes to the small town suburb where his office, and Sharon's, were located. I saw his car at his office and parked where I could watch it without being seen. I was shaking and trying not to cry, feeling like a thief stalking my prey. What I was doing was totally despicable. Here I was, skulking around to spy on my husband, suspecting him of trying to avoid my talking with his accountant. I just knew that he was going to try to see Sharon and be finished with his meeting before I could ever get there. Adrenalin was surging through me as I tried to reconcile my fears with my conscience. I hated being here; I was angry with Michael; I hated this disease that had made us enemies and was thoroughly disgusted with this life of lies. I had never been so miserable, but I was desperate. If I had looked in the mirror at that moment, I wouldn't have known who I was and the mirror probably would have shattered.

Sure enough, at 9:00, he came out of the office and drove away. I started my car and cruised by the local coffee shop to be sure he hadn't gone in for an innocent cup of coffee, actually hoping he would prove my suspicions, and me, wrong. He wasn't there.

I called Sharon's office on my cell phone and asked if Michael were there. He was. "Please tell him that I decided to come early, too, and I'll be right there," I said in a brighter-than-normal voice. Two minutes later I walked through the door. Michael looked at me with a frown on his face but I just smiled and greeted Sharon cheerily, as though none of this were unusual or unplanned. Sharon chatted as she gave Michael his business reports, succeeding in restoring some of my composure. When their business was concluded, I leaned back in the chair and started in.

"Sharon, when Michael decides to retire, how do we take care of something for the business if he's out on the coast?"

Her matter-of-fact reply was, "That's easy enough. He just gives you permission to write a check or to call me if you have a question about something."

I handed her the power of attorney form, saying, "Is this the kind of permission you're talking about?"

She read through it quickly, nodding her head and said, "Well, Mike, this will keep you from packing up your fishing pole and rushing back here for every little thing."

He started to say something, but Sharon interjected, "These are good papers, Mike. Make it easy on yourself. Martha-Lee can call me if there's anything she's not sure about, and you can check in with me any time you like. This makes sense to me." Then, calmly and looking straight at Michael, she handed him the form and a pen. He signed.

As we walked outside, I gave him a brief hug and said, in as normal a voice as I could produce since my throat seemed completely closed up, "I know you're busy. I'll see you when you get home tonight." I turned and walked to my car, not waiting or wanting to hear anything he might say. I waved as I drove away.

Once I got out of the vicinity, I pulled into a parking lot and sat there shaking uncontrollably and trying to breathe. I had just lived through a terribly bad dream, all of my own making. Regardless of the necessity, it still registers in my mind as the worst thing I had ever done in my life. My duplicity, my not trusting him and my sheer audacity were ripping my heart to pieces. The fabric of my character seemed to have unraveled, leaving nothing worthy behind. This time it was not a mirror that was shattered; I was shattered.

I drove home in a fog of uncertainty, dreading the evening at home to come. Believe it or not, nothing was ever said about the events of that day, either that night or ever. I actually slept that night, utterly exhausted. It was a long time before I could assimilate any rational thought about myself or my actions. What had to be done was done, but the reasons didn't erase the regret I felt. I didn't know the person I saw in the mirror any more, and my life with Michael was unrecognizable.

Learning to live with myself had become as hard as living with Michael's Alzheimer's disease. The outcome eventually resolved, as the disease progressed and there were new challenges to face. It was a relief to be able to handle business with the proper legal authority, which is what restored equanimity about my actions. There are even times, in retrospect, that I feel a glimmer of pride that I actually did all those things that seemed to be uncompromisingly disloyal. They were measures necessary for the safety of our lives.

It was comforting, in the end, to remember the words that came to me one day after a discussion about lying in my support group: when love makes you lie, it's not about lying. It's about loving. What you do when your spouse has Alzheimer's may make you question your integrity, your value system and your own character to the point of not knowing who you are. But you don't have to lose yourself if you remember that love is the defining reason for your actions. You can survive living with both sides of Alzheimer's, and your mirror can reflect a recognizable image after all.

CHAPTER SIX

DAY CARE DAZE

What adult day care really means to both of you

Six

DAY CARE DAZE

The morning finally came and I watched the sunlight shimmering weakly through the trees as I stood in the kitchen making our coffee. The sun seemed unsure of its strength, as though it couldn't decide if it would, could, or should make this a typical July day. I could relate to that, because there was a trembling shimmer inside my heart and head with the same question: could I make this a typical day in any way at all?

My husband Michael had Alzheimer's, and I had a career job. This was definitely one of the times when life presents you with colliding circumstances. A head-on collision of difficult decisions about equally important things, about how to keep my job and what to do with Michael, had been gathering momentum for months.

Today was the day of trying something new that could allow me to keep my job or require me to leave it.

Michael was going to day care for his first day today. The company that Michael had owned had finally dwindled to a close and he no longer drove or had a car. It had become clear that he should not be left alone at home during the days when I worked, and there was no way to sustain our lives without my working. Adult day care was the answer for us, though I didn't even know such a thing existed until I joined a support group during the earlier stages of his Alzheimer's disease. Today was going to be a trial run, with my summer schedule allowing flexible hours so that I could pick him up before lunch. My heart was pounding and my brain was spinning, even though he would only be there for about three hours. As I continued to watch the morning sunlight trying to shine through the trees, I thought I couldn't stand it if it started to rain. Please don't add that to the other things I would have to manage that day.

Oddly enough, the fears and doubts about taking my husband to day care were reminiscent of those I had experienced many years before when I took my son to his first day of school. The questions were different but wrapped in the same kind of uncertainty. What if he did something odd, or something inappropriate? What if he wasn't nice or took something that didn't belong to him? What if all the other participants were so different from him that he didn't fit in? It was a day center for frail adults who couldn't stay at home alone, and several of them had Alzheimer's or other dementia-type conditions. I had visited there, knew the staff and the activities that were planned daily, and that it was a warm and accepting place. But the what-ifs just kept repeating in my head, keeping time with the loud beating of my heart.

The planning that had gone into this daycare enrollment had not been easy for me. How in the world did you get someone like Michael to go to a day care center? The disease had progressed to the point that he didn't know he had Alzheimer's or anything else wrong. Toward the end of his independence he sometimes got lost, and once he came home with no house keys and broke a window to get in; but he never acknowledged those things as important or even as having happened at all.

Judy Shotts, the director of the center who to this day I acknowledge as one of the most important people to enter my life, coached me about suggesting to Michael that he might like to volunteer somewhere since he was now retired and I would be going to work every day once the summer was over. Fortunately, he agreed with enthusiasm that this would be a nice thing to do. So, with that initial obstacle passed, today was the first day and the first of new obstacles that then became mine rather than his.

By the end of the week, the morning sun through my kitchen window was a little stronger, exhibiting much less uncertainty of how it would craft the day, but still showing itself with hesitant promise until the aroma and taste of good coffee offered it a chance to shine. For several days, when I arrived at the day care center to take Michael home just after lunch, he was busy clearing away dishes and washing them in the little sink in the little kitchen. He all but ignored me, signaling that he could not be interrupted in his appointed duties. Judy and the staff explained to me, within his hearing, that he was a valuable help and how much they depended on him to help take care of things others couldn't do. They asked him each time we were leaving if they could count on him the next day, and he assured them he would be there. I had not even been sure during these last weeks of summer that I would take him every day, but he made his own choice to go.

What began as a short day away from me extended into the mid-afternoon, because he was busy. Sometimes he was helping someone play Bingo, moving the chip to cover the correct number under the correct letter. It relieved my mind that he still recognized letters and numbers, although this ability faded fairly soon after that and Michael was no longer interested in Bingo. He then took it as his responsibility to sit with a very elderly woman, who was in a special chair with a tray across it to keep her from trying to stand, which she could no longer do without falling. She would become agitated in the afternoons, and Michael would sit in front of her and pat her hands and talk to her, occasionally handing her something to hold that would please her and keep her calm. These were longer days, since he would not leave until her family came to take her home.

Watching his adjustment to day care was gratifying and sad at the same time. I remembered when my young child first went skipping into school without a backward glance, showing me that he wouldn't miss me at all; and I found that some of that forgotten emotion was directly affecting me again. How odd. I was in such a different life place that I didn't recognize for a while that with my child, surprise at not being missed was quickly replaced with pride in his independence and confidence. Independence, confidence and ability were not part of Michael's life as I perceived it. That was a fallacy I carried into the day care center with me. Michael was indeed feeling confident and useful. It was my lack of confidence in him that kept me from seeing the benefit to him that was unfolding. It had been for my need that day care was necessary; certainly he didn't have needs other than safety concerns that day care could address. I thought I was the only one who could or should have to face and deal with his needs.

In contrast to, or perhaps because of, my personal belief that Michael's day care was actually for me, I had a heart-breaking experience fairly soon after recognizing his adjustment to his new life there. I awoke at 3:00 in the morning, crying, and knew with certainty that I had been waiting for them to tell me that Michael really didn't need to be in an adult day care center. And I knew I wasn't going to hear that. He did belong there. He actually was one of those people who couldn't function without supervision. It was a gripping reality that broke my heart. There was no more thread of hope that all this Alzheimer's stuff really didn't have its hold on us yet, and no more denial. There was also no morning sun that day and not for quite some time, at least that I saw. The coffee I drank each morning had no taste and could not quench the dryness in my mouth or give me any energy to face the day. I was going through the motions in a daze.

My full-time schedule as a school principal had resumed at the end of the summer. Several weeks later when I arrived to pick Michael up, he was sitting at a table with a box in front of him, carefully gluing small strips of patterned wrapping paper onto it. He was engrossed and didn't even notice my arrival. Judy invited me into her office and told me that she had shown him this "craft" task that morning and that he had been reluctant to stop even for snacks and lunch. Other than performing his daily self-appointed dish-washing "duty," and since his elderly friend was no longer there, this was the first thing in which he had shown sustained interest. He had not stopped gluing paper on boxes in intricate patterns all day. I was astonished that such a childish activity could seem even mildly interesting to a grown man. After about a week of this ceaseless activity, he turned to me in the car on the way home one afternoon and said, "I can't be late for work tomorrow. I didn't finish wiring that unit today and have to finish before they come in and change the drawing again."

My brain began whirling in a desperate search for meaning, and then I got it: he thought he was looking at a drawing to wire one of the electrical panels he used to build in the manufacturing company that he created when he first moved here. His company, his drawings, his panels for his manufacturing. The colors and patterns on the paper must have represented drawings for the placement of intricate electrical wiring. I knew this was correct, but the relief of understanding what he meant was quickly overcome with dismay. I watched him for several afternoons and felt increasing disbelief that such a brilliant man with a Ph.D. could glue paper on a box with intent interest and not just walk away from something boring and meaningless. How could he possibly think he was looking at a productive task of building something? Anything. But I was measuring the importance of this experience by my own mental standards and not giving him credit for having his own, now unique, vision of productivity and success. I was cast into another daze, and it was painful to think I didn't know how he thought anymore. He was becoming more and more a stranger to me, all precipitated by day care. I couldn't understand it or see the benefit.

Fortunately, two things occurred within a short period of time that finally brought me to a place of acceptance.

On the way home another day, he asked, "Has my boss lady given you my paycheck?"

Totally startled, I was sure that the jig was up, as the saying goes. He was going to find out it was really a day care center and not a job. Not knowing what in the world to say, I simply told him no, but that we would ask her about that the next morning.

When we did so, she turned to him and said, "Oh, Michael, I'm so sorry if I forgot to tell you that we do direct deposit here. Everybody's paycheck goes directly to their bank."

"Oh, well, that's fine then," was his response as he went over to his boxes.

It was absolutely clear to me then that he really thought he worked there, that he thought he was building something, and that he felt productive. It was a huge benefit to him, giving dignity and meaning to his daily life.

The next thing happened when we were leaving the center one late afternoon. A man who was almost non-verbal in a much later stage of Alzheimer's than Michael's, put out his hand as we passed him going to the door.

Michael shook hands and said good-bye, and they smiled at each other.

Once outside, Michael stopped me just beyond the door and said, "Did you see that guy in there? He never used to say a word to me, but now he's my friend." A large lump formed in my throat as tears gathered in my eyes. It was at that moment that I realized Michael didn't have any friends anymore, until now.

The daze I had been in over his being in adult day care cleared. It was not just for me that he was there. It was also very much for him. He now had a new job, a place to work where he made important things for "the company" as he called it, and he had friends. I may not have realized it, but he was leaving me each day with independence and confidence, just as my young child had done. I was in a different place in my life but I felt pride in Michael, too.

There is something in the way we view our commitment to marriage that makes us feel responsible for the other person's happiness. When something goes wrong with our spouse, it is up to us to take care of it and to make it right, even if we have to do it alone. It's our job. It's what our vows mean. And when the "something wrong" is Alzheimer's, it is exhausting in every way possible. I learned, by having no choice, that taking Michael to a safe place during the day not only allowed me to keep my job, but also to keep him at home longer, perhaps, than I would have been able to otherwise. It was not something I was doing **to** him . . . it was something I was doing *for* him, and the benefits were a blessing.

Michael was in day care for almost two years. That wonderful day care that kept him safe, gave him a job, found friends for him, and sent his paycheck directly to the bank. It couldn't be much better than that. Not when you had viewed adult day care through a daze of thinking it was for your convenience, not knowing any of the redeeming qualities for the persons for whom it was designed. That was an illusion only in my mind. I did, in this sensitive place in our marriage, help him find happiness and a useful existence, and it was through adult day care.

For most of the rest of that time in day care, I smiled as I watched the sun shine through my kitchen window, or even watched the rain, as I made the morning coffee; and it had the sweet taste of satisfaction and gratitude. It was another thing along the way, a very significant thing that helped me survive living with both sides of Alzheimer's.

Dedicated with sincere gratitude to the Ruth Sheets Adult Care Center, Raleigh NC

CHAPTER SEVEN

LOST AND FOUND: THE DARKNESS AND THE LIGHT

The loneliness of not being recognized and the joy of a remembered moment

Seven

Lost and Found: The Darkness and the Light

"Who are you, and where are you taking me?" my husband Michael asked, less than twenty minutes from home on the way to our vacation home on the NC Outer Banks. I was driving, and it was hard to maintain my focus on the highway. He had not called me by name for some time, but when he actually asked me who I was, it was dreadfully shocking. As if someone had thrown ice water in my face, my throat closed up and my breathing stopped. My heart seemed to dip down into my feet. Our relationship flashed through my mind like I was experiencing some terrible accident. No matter how well we think we are adapting to living with Alzheimer's, there is something inside us that is the "where there's life, there's hope" syndrome, which had just disintegrated in that moment.

When you live with your spouse through years of the progression of Alzheimer's disease, there are many things that become lost and much time spent in the darkness of uncertainty, dread and depression.

In retrospect, my mind's eye has created an image of how life was during the years of Alzheimer's with Michael. There was a path we followed that was very dim, shadowed by dark clouds overhead; the ground uneven and rocky with stones that caused us to lose our balance and stumble. I was always leading Michael, and I can still feel the warmth of his hand as I kept a firm grasp on it. My pace was slow as I tried to keep from falling while I looked for a safer place. My thoughts were constantly focused on wishing that Michael would just try to keep up and then maybe, sooner or later, he would walk beside me. But no, the reality was that he couldn't . . . would never . . . catch up or keep up. The dark clouds stayed relentlessly over us.

Along this path were many junctures at which I had to stop and acknowledge that we were again at a strange and different place. Deciding how to continue, which way to turn with even less light to illuminate our way, was exhausting. I would look at Michael then, see him smiling at me and waiting patiently for me to continue. I was losing more of him every time and felt aching pain. Each stop seemed to slow him down more, and I had to be careful not to lose my hold on him altogether. I would grip his hand tighter and trudge on, with the pain of loss coursing through me. It was this latest juncture where I lost my identity, when Michael didn't know who I was anymore. Who was I? Who was he?

Continuing on our trip to the coast, I had little, if any conversation. It took all my energy and concentration to drive, with my emotions threatening to overtake me as each mile passed beneath us. When we boarded the ferry that crossed the Pamlico Sound, Michael slept in the car while I just leaned my head back and kept my eyes closed. The constant cries of the sea gulls gave an audible form to the silent cries of my heart that were threatening to burst forth. The deep throbbing of the engines thrummed through my body in a visceral response to the pain I was desperately holding inside. I didn't know what to say or how to talk to this man who was my husband, but who didn't know me. I kept hoping, however, that he would remember everything again once we got to our vacation house. He had built that house many years before and loved being there more than anywhere else in the world. Surely he would know then where we were and who I was.

Hoping did not make it happen. His not knowing me continued the several days we were there. I spent a lot of time in the bathroom sobbing and just as much time getting myself together to come out. I learned later that I also did and said things while we were there that I had no memory of doing. I was in a paralyzed state of shock.

After what seemed like an interminable time there, returning home did not bring his memory of who I was back. Somehow, I knew it wouldn't. So began a new phase of feeling hopeless in my struggle to live with Alzheimer's. His constantly asking me my name, if I were just visiting, if I were married, if I had a family, and where did I live, was the most difficult adjustment I had had to make. Poignantly, he asked me several times over the next couple of years if I would consider marrying him. It made me feel proud but was no real solace. I missed him deeply, this man I had married. It was at this time that I found the words "the other side of Alzheimer's." The disease was Michael's, but I saw clearly that it had a side that was changing me, and it was deeply painful.

During those months and years, I saw a wonderful counselor and attended a support group of people who had, currently or in the past, a family member with dementia. Probably the main reason I managed to keep from falling into an even darker place of despair was this support group. There were always helpful suggestions to avoid conflict, to encourage difficult decisions that were for safety and welfare, and how to communicate with other family members who lived elsewhere.

Sometimes in one of these meetings, someone would describe something that had the others saying how wonderful it was to "savor the moments whenever possible." I had no idea what that meant or how it would feel, because there were no good moments to savor in my opinion. Even if there were a momentary breakthrough of memory, it certainly wouldn't last and would leave you feeling even sadder than before. Having a moment to savor was just not possible. Until it happened to me.

Before Michael's illness had progressed very far, my younger sister who lived in another part of the country was diagnosed with breast cancer. I was terribly afraid of losing her and felt dreadful that I couldn't be with her. Sometimes after talking with her on the phone, I would just sit down and cry.

One day after Michael had stopped knowing who I was, we had just left a place that was familiar to us but I knew he hadn't recognized where we were at all. I was feeling depressed and unutterably lonely.

All of a sudden he asked me what my name was, and after I told him, he turned to me and said, "You have a sister, don't you?"

I answered that I had two sisters, to which he replied, "Yes, but one of them lives a long way away."

I was in disbelief as I affirmed it, and then he said, "There is something wrong with her that makes you cry."

There was a stunned silence from me before I could say a word, and what was happening became in that instant my "moment to savor." In that one brief exchange, he gave himself back to me. He knew me. He remembered something that had been extremely important to me and connected with me in a way that was once again deeply meaningful to our relationship.

When I told him that she was over her illness and doing well, his eyes filled with tears as he patted my hand and said, "Thank goodness. I'm so glad."

I knew he was with me in that moment and that he cared. I was still in disbelief but was experiencing a sense of sheer joy. The dark clouds overhead dissipated, letting in an incredible amount of sunshine that filled my entire being. The light that had been so dim for so long was bright. His words had leapt from my ears to my brain, then to my heart and into my memory. There were still rocks in the path under our feet, but the painfully jagged edges were smoother and I was never as unsteady and off balance again.

Of course that moment didn't last, but it didn't matter. My heart was filled with gratitude when I had forgotten what gratitude even was. My memory stored that moment forever. I still feel the warmth of the wonder that spread through me then, any time I think of it. For the rest of Michael's life, even as he continued to decline, I never forgot how that moment restored something to our relationship that was loving, when I thought he would never know me to love me again. He had, in fact, found my identity and handed it gently back to me, shining a light on this juncture on our path. He could not have given me a more precious gift. That moment brought the power of peace and strength, and I never again felt that my identity was lost. It was wrapped securely and lovingly in a special bright place in my heart marked "savor the moments whenever you can."

If you are stumbling in the darkness of living with this disease, please remember that at some time, when you have no hope of being touched again by feelings of recognition and love, a moment to savor may come along your path. What you thought was forever lost will be forever found. Store it safely in your heart; it will be one thing that will not be forgotten.

It will help you find peace, too, and the strength to survive living with Alzheimer's and the pain of the other side, too.

CHAPTER EIGHT

JUDGE WITHOUT A JURY

*Feelings when your spouse goes through
paranoia with Alzheimer's*

Eight

JUDGE WITHOUT A JURY

"Michael, are you ready yet?" I called up the stairs to my husband for the third time. No answer, although I could hear movement and muttering. I reached the landing, turned left into the bedroom and saw him sitting on the side of the bed, fully dressed but barefoot. Every sock from his dresser was spread out around him, as he methodically counted each one and stacked them neatly in a pile. Or three.

"Are you ready to go yet?" I repeated, even though the scene gave me my answer.

"I know damn well I had more socks than this yesterday. Where the hell are they?" he demanded in his recently acquired voice of accusation. This was the third time this week that he had become obsessed with the idea that someone had been hiding his socks, or very probably stealing them, and he was not pleased.

Here we go again, I thought to myself, as I struggled once again to find an answer that would satisfy him. Why did I always feel guilty? The power of his paranoia, one of the symptoms of his Alzheimer's disease, was such that I invariably felt guilty of removing, hiding, or stealing whatever was missing at the moment. I quickly searched my mind about leaving some of the laundry in the dryer or about discarding socks with holes in the toes. No. There was no answer, really. I had tried them all with no success.

The only thing I could do now was to say, "I really don't know where they are, but let me help you put the ones you still have back in the drawer while you finish getting ready to go. We'll look into it when we get home from work tonight."

One of the saddest and most frustrating things about living with your spouse who has Alzheimer's is that you have little, if any, control over the ideas that seem to come from nowhere at any given moment. You certainly have no ready answers most of the time for the questions that always sound like accusations. For several days before the episodes of missing socks, it had been the daily question about missing money. It was his routine each night to empty his pockets of loose change and put it on top of his dresser, but there was always some of it missing the next morning.

"Have you taken some of my money? I know I'm supposed to have more than this," he would say, as he waved his hand around and looked straight at me with a scowl and furrowed brow. My reaction was worse with the money than with the socks, just because it was money. I couldn't help that instant of feeling guilty, no matter how hard I tried and how certain I was that I had never even thought of taking money off his dresser. Some things just don't seem to have an explanation, and his missing amount of change was definitely one of those. There was no answer that didn't sound like an excuse at best and a lie at worst.

I finally learned just to say, "No, I don't need any money today, thank you," and walk on downstairs. Now that the socks were frequently missing, I found myself wanting to grin and say, *Maybe the people who stole your change have decided to take your socks instead*, but of course I didn't. That might have been a humorous response in previous times, when honest mistakes might have made us laugh, but not now. Not when Alzheimer's had turned even insignificant things into unfortunate confrontations. He was the judge; I, the obvious prime suspect with no reasonable defense. My exasperation over being late, yet again, in getting him to his adult day care center and me to my job, was expressed only in my silent tension and sense of futility.

There had been many incidents during this phase of Alzheimer's that were unpleasant. Michael had never been a person who was distrustful, as are some people who always seem to look for ulterior motives in things said or done. His had been an engaging personality, and he was far quicker to see the humor in a situation than insincerities. To be suspicious of even the smallest details and irregularities had been a very difficult phase of his personality change to accept.

"Watch out, watch out, the police are behind us!" he would warn constantly as I was driving somewhere with him in the passenger seat vigilantly watching the side-view mirror. Even a pick-up truck with a ladder on top would trigger this panic. Pizza delivery cars with the signs on the roof became ruthless law enforcement vehicles following our every move. My relaxation breathing techniques while driving were often over-taxed in any fifteen minute period, converting relaxation into exasperation.

Recalling the period and power of his paranoia, I realize in retrospect that the worst of these episodes often took place in the mornings in our bedroom-turned-courtroom.

"Who the hell do these pants belong to?" was his demand one morning as he stepped out of his closet holding a pair of faded charcoal grey pants on the hanger. Swinging them in front of me as I was fixing my hair at the dresser mirror, he was angrier than I had ever seen him. My face in the mirror turned ashen.

I turned toward him and said quickly, "Those are yours, Michael."

He raised his voice: "The hell they are. I've never seen these pants in my life. Now tell me *who the hell do they belong to?*"

The judge stood there in a threatening stance, there was no jury, and I was already guilty and stunned into silence. The blood that had drained from my face flooded my heart as it beat rapidly.

My thoughts raced from one split-second response to another, while I stammered things like, "All the pants in your closet are yours, honey. There are nobody's clothes in there but yours!"

Still swinging them in front of me, he said in a deadly calm voice that rang with certainty, "Don't lie to me. These are not my pants."

Desperately, I answered, "You haven't worn them in so long I guess you forgot you had them."

It was a classic stand-off. We stood there staring at each other, the judge and the suspect, and then I remembered: the person with Alzheimer's is always right. No exceptions. My support group had taught me the rule when facing a confrontation to stop arguing, because you can never change a person's mind when he or she is always right.

Taking a deep breath, as unsteady as it was, I forced out the words, "I don't have any idea whose pants those are."

And then I didn't breathe until I saw the anger fade from his face and he said, "Oh." He walked back into his closet and hung up the pants.

Court had adjourned, the gavel laid to rest on the judge's bench. But the verdict wasn't clear to me. After taking him into the day care center later, I walked back out to the car and the tears came. I had been shaken to the core. My feelings were deeply hurt; I was angry and totally devastated. My husband, my marriage, and my life had seemed to crumble even more in that dreadful confrontation. My heart broke at the idea that he had actually thought I was responsible for some other man's pants being in his closet, with all the unsavory implications that must have meant to him. I couldn't accept that. I felt utterly defeated, as the essence of our happiness disintegrated in my mind. I had never considered the possibility that he would think I could disregard the sanctity of marriage, and the pain of discovering that possibility was overwhelming. At that moment I couldn't even be angry with Alzheimer's disease, which was a reasonable verdict to the trial. It was still Michael who had thought I was guilty of infidelity, and I was truly angry with him. Damn the whole mess: him and his suspicious thoughts. As I sobbed out my loss of love, I did understand that it was Alzheimer's that had been the judge that morning. Alzheimer's had no need for a jury. But my heart wept because I hadn't had even the benefit of doubt. I had truly been a victim of Alzheimer's, that dreadful other side, and I didn't have to like it regardless of understanding it.

It was a long time before I could move beyond the pain and focus once more on each new day and each new challenge. It was a long time before I could accept the truth that Alzheimer's was the cruel enemy and not Michael. There was no way to change what had happened, and that memory left a scar on my heart. But I had to move on and ignore the tendency to keep replaying it in my mind, which would only have clouded my judgments in dealing with future incidents.

The next difficult stage began one morning when Michael came downstairs for his coffee. "Who were all those people here last night?" he asked.

Surprised at the question, I asked in return, "Where?"

"Here, in the house. Did you enjoy the party?"

Falling into the habit of disclaiming, I said, "There wasn't a party here last night. There was nobody here but you and I."

"There most certainly was," he said, adding, "I didn't want to interrupt, so I stayed in the bedroom."

"Maybe you were dreaming," I suggested.

"That was no dream. There was a party here. I just wanted to know who all the people were."

Suddenly realizing that we were having one of those conversations that was bordering on a confrontation, I moved away from the dining room table, emptied my cup in the sink and said, "I have to get dressed for work. So do you when you finish your coffee."

Upstairs, I began the daily routine of turning the shower on for him, knowing he would follow me up immediately. I had begun fixing the water temperature ever since the day he almost scalded himself. I readied the shampoo to pour in his hand to show him how to rub it on his head, all the while puzzling what he could have heard to make him think other people had been in the house the night before. No more was said about it as we readied ourselves for the day and left the house.

The next morning was a repeat scene. He asked again about the people who had been there during the night, and I just replied that we had not had company and avoided further conversation. Thinking about it all through the day, I resolved to watch carefully all the television shows we would see that evening, and did so. On the third morning when he asked the same question, I was even more perplexed. No television show the evening before had had a party scene, or even a scene with a large gathering of any kind. Again, I made as brief an answer as I could, and he didn't mention it again . . . until the next morning. This continued day after day, with my remaining clueless as to the trigger for his thinking.

One night he was so convinced that people were in the house that he got up twice to check around. Of course I got up each time he did. He had been through a stage thinking it was time to go to work in the middle of the night and would go outside to look for his ride. (Not that he ever had someone come and pick him up for anything; I took him every day to the day center where he thought he worked.) Some nights I could persuade him to come back in the house and wait since it was not time yet for his ride, and we would doze in living room chairs until morning. Some nights I managed to persuade him to go back upstairs and lie on the bed until it was time to go, but sleep then for me didn't happen even after he would fall sound asleep again. Now he was getting up at night to see who was having a party in our house. He always seemed to think that I was in the middle of the merriment, not sleeping next to him in the bed. Mornings after his nightly checks still brought on the same questions, and they were becoming more and more demanding.

After weeks of this, he began to ask even before bedtime if people were going to be coming to our house. When I would say that nobody was expected, he would just shake his head and grumble, "We'll see about that."

People always came. He always got up more than once each night to patrol the house (not going outside anymore, thank goodness,) and I was getting less and less sleep. As the principal of a small school, I had a lot of responsibility and had always enjoyed the people with whom I interacted each day, but daily interactions became a struggle. I was tired, distracted and worried.

Wondering what would work to solve this night-visitors problem, I came up with the idea one night to try something new. As we started upstairs to bed, sure enough he asked about people coming for a party.

I said, "I have an idea. Would it make you feel better if I sleep down here on the couch by the front door? That way if anyone comes, I can wake you up and we'll decide what to do about it."

He turned to me with a look of wonder and said, "Would you do that?"

Answering that I would be glad to, I gathered the necessary things to make up the couch, messing around until he was in bed and asleep. I spent three sleepless nights on the couch, which was the length-of-my-feet too short for comfort, listening for him to get up. He did not get up, but each morning he came down and asked me if I had had a good time at the party. It wasn't solving any problem, and it was creating more fatigue for me.

At my support group meeting that week, by coincidence, it was pointed out that sometimes when even family members come into a home unexpectedly, the person with Alzheimer's will think they are intruders and have been known to attack them. In a flash, I realized the danger of the situation in which I had placed myself. What if Michael came downstairs during the night and saw me lying on the couch without knowing who I was? Would he attack? Would he throw me out the door? I knew then that I shouldn't continue that plan. Not that it was working, anyway.

The problem did not resolve, by my efforts or anything else. It was then that I began to think that maybe I couldn't go on this way. Mine was the only income. Michael's social security could not meet all our expenses, no matter how careful I could be. I had to work. My friends and family, particularly my son Matt, began asking me if I had a plan for placing Michael in a secure facility. With decreasing physical strength, I felt my emotional strength wearing thin.

It was when the leader of my support group told me that Matt had called her from his home in Minneapolis and said, "Tell me how to help my mom," that I knew my situation was going beyond me. She told me point blank that he was afraid he was losing me, and he was watching both of us lose Michael.

It was not long after that when Matt called and said, "Mom, I want you to have a plan for Michael. It doesn't have to be a plan for tomorrow, but I want you to have a plan soon."

The greatest fear yet took over: the fear of giving up on Michael. But there was also the fear of not being able to survive this journey through Alzheimer's. With encouragement through counseling, my support group, and my son and family, I began looking for a facility placement. I went through the process with the distant thought that it would someday be time to turn Michael's care over to a place where he would be safe and respected, that it would become time to let go, and time for me to rest or I might not be there for him as long as he needed me. I did it without feeling the emotional impact of placing him anytime soon.

As I conclude telling about this chapter in our lives, I recall a conversation that Michael and I had had many years before when we were getting to know each other and discussing the experience each of us had had being widowed. Michael told me that you always have the scar of losing your husband or wife, but the scar heals enough with time so that you can touch it without fear of pain. You can touch it, it's tender, but you do not have to recoil from it. It is always a part of you, but it is *part* of your life experience rather than the whole of your experience. On this he was right. I will add that there are scars left also at the end of the journey through Alzheimer's. Only by remembering the love that bound you together in the first place can the rough, painful edges of the scars begin to smooth over.

The fingertips of your mind learn to touch the scars gently, with no pressure, and the judge without a jury moves to the background of your memory. The trial is over. You did, in fact, survive living with Alzheimer's, and with the other side of it.

READY FOR THE HOLIDAYS

What to expect, or not, for holiday time

Nine

Ready for the Holidays

Christmas was twenty days away and I was ready to put holiday decorations around the house. Standing on a chair in the spare bedroom closet, I chose the first of several medium-sized boxes to begin to uncover the treasures packed away eleven months ago. Looking over my shoulder, ready to hand the box to my husband Michael, I saw that he was not there. He had come upstairs with me, perfectly willing to help, but I took too long deciding which box to select first and he forgot why he was standing there. Alzheimer's is not a convenient companion for holiday preparations.

"Michael, where are you? Will you please come here?" I called, hoping that I wouldn't have to get off the chair to go find him.

Luckily, he followed the sound of my voice and returned. Handing him the box, I pointed to the bed as the place he should put it and watched as he set it down and left the room. I chose the next box to lift down and called to him again. It worked for that box, but for the remaining two, I had to climb down off the chair and go get him. He was busy examining and rearranging things on the top of his dresser in our bedroom across the hall. Once he started that kind of activity, it was hard to redirect him. It had taken three times as long to get boxes off the closet shelf as I thought it would. It had been a long day and I found my energy for enjoying holiday decorating waning fast.

When any holiday approaches, it almost always is accompanied by its favorite best friend: stress. Stress comes shrewdly disguised as fewer hours and more demands in the day, and less to show for all the cramming of your best efforts into stretching time and yourself to the limit.

Finding time for holiday preparations in the best of circumstances, when you know what has to be done, where and how to do it, is still a troublesome part of the process. The feeling of excitement and pleasure is pushed aside too often in favor of much needed rest and not staying up late at night. The saving grace most of the time is when you realize that you can still make things nice and create an atmosphere for your family and friends to enjoy even when you settle for less than you originally planned. Maybe you have only two pies instead of three, your table is decorated but not the two front windows, and you totally forgot to find your little simmering pot that creates the heavenly scent of cinnamon or citrus or the deep, deep woods.

Holiday preparations when your spouse has Alzheimer's disease are even more challenging. In any home, holidays can often become complicated by different opinions and preferences between spouses. In the presence of Alzheimer's, though, coming home after work, knowing what task you want to accomplish and mark off your list, can turn an evening into a less than happy atmosphere. When Michael could not remember where I was if I walked into the next room, he would follow me around and ask what I was doing several times in fewer than several minutes. Except, of course, when I needed him to stand near me to take a box of decorations out of my hands. Waiting seemed to require more time than his memory could handle, and he would wander away. The effect on me was that I lost any continuity or semblance of organization that I thought I had. Frustration and impatience are heavy enough wrapped around your shoulders, but add a large amount of guilt for being impatient on top of that and you've got trouble. It's your own trouble; not his, because he doesn't know a holiday is coming.

That's the dilemma: he doesn't know a holiday is coming, but you do. Why are preparations even necessary?

Why bother adding all that fuss and rush to an already stressful daily life? Mostly it's because it's what you do in a normal existence, and shrugging it off has a feeling of giving up. Maybe it's the tenacity of spirit but why should you refrain from finding and fixing the beauty that you enjoy and instead resign yourself with defeat to a life you have but don't want? Giving up was a concept that I rejected. Ignoring the holidays doesn't mean they don't come. It just means that getting ready for them may require being a bit creative as you find the patience you need to do it.

For the past two years, Christmas at our house had been a strain, culminating in more than needing help getting decorations out of the closet. This year I figured out that I couldn't physically, alone, put up a live six-foot tree such as the ones we always had and I didn't think Michael would know how to do it any more. And I had better not take him with me to select one, because he would wander away if I were talking with anyone else. So I asked a neighbor to take me to get a tree and help put it in the house while Michael was in day care. With no time to decorate it after it was in the house, I brought Michael home that afternoon at the end of the day.

Believe it or not, he didn't even mention it until later that evening, when he casually asked, "Why is there a tree in here with us?"

I smiled and explained it was our Christmas tree and that I would decorate it tomorrow, which seemed to satisfy his curiosity but not engage his interest at all.

The hardest part became the confusion created by television commercials. Michael finally connected our brightly decorated tree with all the commercials showing people giving and unwrapping gifts around a Christmas tree. After several days, Michael began worrying about not having bought me a Christmas present.

He'd lean forward in his chair during a commercial and say with great distress, "But I don't have a present for you!"

So, shopping we went, several times. I would buy a little something while we were at the corner drug store or some small place, wrap it and put it under the tree. Then the next time he'd get upset, I would pick it up and show him the tag which said it was to me, "from Michael." It didn't work. He never remembered any of our shopping trips or any of the packages. I finally removed all presents from under the tree after he was asleep one night, and when he would react to those commercials settled on telling him that we would do our Christmas shopping over the weekend.

This was the first year there were no family visits, since Michael's children were traveling and my son Matt was on a skiing trip. This turned out to be fortunate since group gatherings had become confusing and stressful for Michael, with difficulty following conversations and remembering names. We had a peaceful time, watching his favorite television shows on tape and eating a quiet Christmas dinner on trays in the living room. It would not have been my choice had there been an alternative, but Alzheimer's disease, our constant companion, at least remained in the background for the most part, for the day.

Valentine's Day, coming on the heels of Christmas, was special to me for us, but had me groping for some way to celebrate it that wouldn't be upsetting to Michael. I didn't dare purchase a gift for him, but I did buy a beautiful card and plan a special dinner with candlelight, a tradition we had started even before we were married. This year it was just the two of us, having dinner at home with a glass of wine to toast our love. The chocolate dessert, one of his favorites, was the only thing that you could have called a gift. There is no denying that I had to fight down the sad realization that Michael had no idea what the occasion was. It was one of the loneliest days I had spent yet. He was right there with me, but he wasn't really there at all. I wasn't even sure if he knew who I was. Watching several television shows that night of lost-and-found love stories gave a perfect excuse for my tears.

Another year passed and this one found me getting out a few Christmas decorations that I had packed away in easy-to-lift paper grocery bags with handles. I didn't have the nerve to say no to my neighbor when he offered once again to take me to get a tree. (Why is it that you never want to admit that your problem still lingers, that it might even be worse, or that you haven't managed to find some miraculous way to keep it from affecting your life?) I had thought I might just get a small artificial table tree, but I didn't know how to refuse my neighbor's offer without sounding as though I didn't care about the holiday. The difference this year was that I chose an even smaller tree, and I took time to decorate it before picking Michael up from day care that afternoon.

"Look at this!" was Michael's delighted exclamation when I unlocked the door and opened it that evening, flipping on the switch that lighted the tree just as he was coming in.

"That's the most beautiful thing I've ever seen!" He was thrilled, as though he had never seen a Christmas tree in his life. He walked around it, examining the ornaments and talking with enthusiasm about the lights that I had strung on it almost to excess. It was colorful and gay, to say the least. I never again made the mistake of confusing or distressing him with gifts under the tree. I had learned that lesson all too well the year before.

Christmas was here again, and this year I was ready. For days, I carefully showed only taped favorite television shows instead of commercial programming. Our evenings were peaceful, just as the season should be.

Imagine, if you can, coming in the door each and every day to find a brand new tree, decorated with colorful ornaments and lights, welcoming you home. That's what that Christmas was: a new tree every day, a lovely surprise. Alzheimer's gave Michael a new experience each day instead of remembering that what you saw was the same thing you saw yesterday. It was always new. It was a new experience for me, too, to smile when we got home every afternoon. How simple life can be . . . sometimes.

In February, with Valentine's Day approaching, I was ready for it, too. I had accepted that it would be a day like any other for Michael, even though I would serve a special dinner and include his favorite chocolate dessert. This year, I realized that the calendar was not responsible for a celebration of commitment. Michael and I were together, albeit in a different way and a different place in our lives. But it was still our life together, and I could celebrate the love I felt for him without decorations, presents or declarations. Deep inside, my heart knew that he felt love, too, from me and for me. My loneliness was still there, as always, but love for each other was our common bond.

Finding the feelings, love and peace with what is, is the only real way to get ready for the holidays. It's the only real way to survive living with both sides of Alzheimer's.

THANK GOODNESS IT'S MONDAY

The difficulties of weekends without the regular work week schedule

Ten

Thank Goodness it's Monday

———————

T, G, I, and F are still favorite letters of the alphabet, although other abbreviations of texting vie for the same status of popularity. TGIF, said as a word, still begins reverberating throughout the work place along about Thursday afternoon. Smiles appear on stressed faces, humor finds its way back into conversation and thoughts of work move aside to let images of leisure pleasure share the cerebral space. Not so, however, if your spouse has Alzheimer's disease and the week-day accommodations are suspended for two long days. Weekends can be more stressful than the work week. Waking up on Friday mornings is more likely to trigger an Oh, No, It's Friday, rather than a TGIF.

When my husband Michael's Alzheimer's disease had progressed to the point that he was enrolled in an adult day care center Monday through Friday so that I could continue working, it came as a surprise to learn that weekends were no longer for relaxing or having fun. Managing our time on weekends was an exercise in trial and error, with "trial" being the operative word, accompanied by "tribulation" added to the "error."

Thankfully, he had become convinced that the day center was where he worked, which was a blessing during the week. What became difficult was his confusion when we did not leave the house on Saturdays and Sundays to go to work. He was restless and agitated; he paced, was sometimes argumentative and was not satisfied with anything to do around the house. He did love working in the yard, but his recognition of things that were planted on purpose and those growing wild left a lot to be desired. I had to channel his energy for raking to the areas behind the flower garden, just at the edge of the woods. There was a sizeable space not heavily wooded, filled with scraggly little trees, hearty under-the-surface vines and dark dirt that always smelled damp, mostly because it always was. There were leaves galore to rake and Michael actually crafted paths suitable for walking that looked almost professionally landscaped. Far too many weekend days, though, the weather was not conducive to outside labor and those were the days that gave me a great deal of trouble.

Searching for solutions to occupy him, I decided that I could take him grocery shopping with me, which was my usual routine on Saturdays during the years he still worked in his office. He would willingly go with me, but the grocery store was not a familiar or favorite place of his. He did like pushing the cart, which became his job while I tried to walk slightly ahead to look for needed items on the shelves. The aisles beckoned to him as a raceway might and he pushed that cart as though it were a vehicle with a destination mission. It soon became a challenge for me to be quick enough to keep up with him. He had no idea that the cart was actually to hold the items I chose. I tried gathering several things before running to catch up with him, but sometimes he would have turned two or three aisles over, and it was awkward to hold things without dropping at least two of them while I searched for him. It was not an altogether happy solution and actually became worse, forcing me to admit this was not the way to have a pleasant Saturday morning.

On one particular Saturday, it was cold and blustery as only Saturdays can be when you need them to be warm and sunny. It was also one of those days when the household was out of many staples, and I had a long grocery list. After entering the store and giving Michael the cart, we started down the first aisle. I was, as usual, feeling the need to rush to find the things we needed before he got out of sight.

I saw the first item, grabbed it off the shelf and put it in the cart. I started walking quickly on ahead, only to be stopped by Michael's loud voice saying, "Wait a minute . . . . did you PAY for that?" Since that was the first time I think he had ever noticed what I put in the cart, I was a little startled, not just at his words but at the unmistakable indignation in his voice.

I returned to him and said quietly, "I'll pay for everything when we're finished."

I think I recall that he let me put one more thing in the cart unchallenged, but that was it. The next item had him exclaiming again, "Did you PAY for that?"

I did my utmost to shhshh him, smiling at people walking by, but it did no good whatsoever. All of a sudden this time his attention was entirely on me putting things in the cart, and I admit I would far rather he have driven his race cart around the cart-track. The third time he demanded to know if I had "paid for that," I realized that getting him quiet was not going to work.

I began answering him in as loud a voice as I had nerve to use, "We pay for everything at the same time before we leave."

Heads were turning in our direction, and I was sorry that I was wearing a coat. The word "shoplifting" seemed to be flashing in neon lights over my head. Stuffing goods down the front of my coat, or in the pockets, or anywhere to conceal my groceries was obviously my game. Even though I was embarrassed for him, I was quickly becoming mortified for myself. It was dreadful. Taking a chance that I could at least get the urgent things on the list before uniformed officers, brandishing weapons of course, arrived on the scene, I pulled the cart—and Michael—behind me to one or two other places in the store.

I showed him each thing I picked up before putting it in the cart and said firmly, "I'm putting this in the cart so we can pay for it in a minute."

Again, I spoke in as loud a voice as I had nerve to use, although to my ears it sounded pretty false, indeed. As crowded as that store is on Saturdays and as many times as I had shopped there, I saw not one employee I recognized or who could possibly have recognized me.

There was no one there who could testify that I was not a habitual thief, even though I had a husband who was determined to steer me away from a life of crime. Trial and error and tribulation. Oh, no, it's Saturday. Need I say that that was the last time Michael went grocery shopping with me?

Other things I tried on weekends were equally unsuccessful, albeit not publicly humiliating. I finally asked the director of his day care center if I could bring home some of the crafts and tasks he enjoyed doing at the center, but that was a miserable failure, too. He had no idea what or how to do those things at home. He simply could not transfer his recognition of them to a different location. I finally realized that this was in line with the phenomenon of not knowing where they are when you take a person with Alzheimer's away from a familiar place. The farther away you get, the more disoriented and confused they get. Work items from day care were forgotten tasks at home, certainly not things that kept him occupied.

For the most part, weekends when we could not be in the back yard became days to suffer through the best way we could. It was difficult to maintain my patience with his pacing, following me every step I took, and asking the same questions countless times.

When I lost my temper and spoke sharply to him, "Will you please just sit down and wait for me to finish making lunch," I felt dreadful and defeated. It was exhausting. He slept in front of the television a lot, which made me feel guilty for not finding things to stimulate and occupy him, but I had no energy to do anything else. Maybe like shoplifting, I suppose guilt is something to which you adapt when the need is there. I had taped the only shows he seemed to understand; and before it was over, I could recite every line from every "M*A*S*H" and every "JAG" ever shown. At least these were shows I enjoyed, too, for the first fifty times, anyway. Gratitude for peaceful hours, though, always took the sting out of boredom. Would it ever be Monday again?

Other than bad weather weekends, the worst staying-at-home weather experience I can report is the one when we had an ice storm that left us without power for more than three days, even though it was not confined to actual weekend days. As the house got colder and more uncomfortable, I started wearing my coat and knit hat over all my sweatshirts, and I dressed Michael in layers also. Long-sleeved knit shirts and v-neck sweaters were under his coat, and I tried my best to keep his knit hat on his head. Several times a day, I brought him into the dining room next to the glass patio door, where we sat and watched the birds hopping, fluttering and sliding around for the seed I had tossed out the door. But after a couple of minutes of this, he would get up and start to go out the front door.

Jumping up, I would hold his arm and say, "No, no, we can't go outside. There is ice all over the ground and we could fall and get hurt."

He would look at me and say, in a confused voice, "But these are my going outside clothes."

I would lead him back to the dining room and try to offer him some cheese and crackers and fruit. That didn't work, because you don't sit down at the dining table to eat with your coat and hat on. I gave up on the idea of eating at the table when we were fully clothed as for a winter's hike. Most of the cold collations I served were eaten standing in the kitchen or from tray tables in the living room, which was a common thing to do when there was television to watch. Having no electricity created, indeed, days of trial and tribulation. Michael would doze off while waiting for a show to appear on the screen, and his patience with me for not turning it on certainly eclipsed mine with the entire situation.

We'd go upstairs to bed when it got dark, and fortunately Michael would go to sleep right away. I would try to read, holding a flashlight while doing that awkward trick of balancing my book on my knees. I was extra alert during these nights, because if Michael got up in the total darkness, I knew he'd be lost. We had nightlights all over the house, but only the kind that turn on with electricity, much to my chagrin.

On the third day of this ice-bound misery, I heard on the battery-powered radio that one of the fast food places nearby was open, with a long line of cars around it and down the highway. That was it. I made up my mind that we were going to get in that line, no matter what. I had poured salt on the front porch and steps and began praying that we could get to the car without mishap. I would have carried Michael to the car by then, I was so desperate for a way to keep him warm. Just as we were getting ready to go outside, in our going-outside clothes, the phone rang.

It was the director of his day care center, saying the center had power, and she was inviting any families who were in the cold and dark to come down there to stay.

"Bring blankets and sleeping bags if you have them, and whatever food you have that we can cook," were her instructions. "Remember there are showers, too."

"We're going to work," I told Michael when I got off the phone. "I have to take some things with us, so wait for me to get ready."

I gathered bedding, towels, toothbrushes, soap and shampoo, and then looked for food. A box of spaghetti noodles, an unopened jar of pasta sauce, oatmeal cookies, and a package of hamburger that had just begun thawing in the freezer were my contributions to the cause.

Michael had sat down in his chair while I was busy, and I realized that I would need to make several trips to the car with supplies before we could actually leave. I also wanted to test the trek outside without him, so I turned and said, in a very stern voice, "Don't get up. Don't come out the door yet. I'll be right back. Wait." I must have sounded like I meant business, because he didn't get out of the chair.

The day was bright and sunny, despite the cold temperature, and the major roads had been made marginally passable by drivers obviously more adventurous than I, and some limited scraping. Some cars had even made tracks in the neighborhood roads, and I made it to the main thoroughfare without a problem, except for my heart being in my throat. Michael never mentioned the icy, white scene, although he knew we were going to work and it was probably as much a relief to him as to me, although for different reasons.

I have never felt more gratitude in my life as we made our way to the center. Never. We were going to a place where it was warm, there would be lights and friends, and we could eat hot food and actually take showers. But by far the most important part was that it was a place Michael knew; he was comfortable there and had things to do that were "his work."

I shall always remember when we arrived and Judy, his "boss lady," met us at the door, Michael saying "I never thought I'd be called back in to work on the weekend."

But he said it with pride and walked straight over to the place that was his work station and began organizing the things that kept him interested each day; those things he did not know how to do at home. He worked steadily until a hot meal was ready, and we ate with relaxed camaraderie and calm conversation around us. If Heaven had opened up to welcome us, it could not have been a better place to be. He slept on the infirmary bed that night, and I slept on blankets on the floor beside him. The "weekend" trials and tribulations were just memories. We were warm, safe and with friends who knew and accepted Michael just as he was; and I said heartfelt prayers of gratitude. It would only be a couple of more days before our normal routine returned, when I could say, "Thank goodness it's Monday," regardless of the day of the week.

Weekends, while undoubtedly the hardest times, were not the only difficult hours of daily life. Evenings were long and lonely, largely spent void of conversation and watching television. Conversation is one of the big blank spots in your life when your spouse has Alzheimer's disease, which leaves a hole in your heart and spirit. "Thank goodness for television" ranks right up there with "thank goodness it's Monday," even when the person with Alzheimer's has a limited scope of interest that does not include many things that you would rather see.

The evening of September 11, 2001, like all other Americans, Michael and I sat in front of the television watching the unbelievable sights and sounds. It was doubly horrific to me, because I had learned early in the day that my niece was in the Pentagon when it was hit. An Air Force officer, she was in the safest place she could possibly be in the building and was unhurt, airlifted with armed services commanders to an undisclosed location. Finding out, hours later, that she was safe was a huge relief but did not completely ease my overwhelmingly chaotic feelings. I did not try to discuss it or even comment on it to

Michael as we watched the endless replays and continuous real-life drama. I wasn't sure if my emotions about this tragedy would upset him, confuse him, or if he could even understand that it was the news rather than a television show. It took about three days, maybe longer, for it to become something he realized that had really happened in our present day world, and that it was about America.

He looked up at tall buildings one morning when we were driving downtown to his day care center and said, "Well, at least they missed these!"

We had not been talking about it, of course, but I knew instantly what he meant. The feeling I had at that moment was one of deep appreciation that we could share, in some way, this huge nightmare. Because it is difficult after a certain stage of Alzheimer's to separate fantasy from reality, it had not been surprising that he had never mentioned the tragedy during the countless hours we had seen it on television, and I didn't expect him to understand that this was a current event. Watching it and suffering, though, had been very lonely for me, as though we were living in different worlds far removed from the one we used to share.

It was another couple of nights later, when we were again watching the news, that he leaned forward in his chair and took my hand. He said, very seriously, "You know I have to go back to the Air Force now."

What a remarkable return to the present: his understanding that something was threatening us and he needed to be part of the protection. He had been a decorated fighter pilot in WWII, he loved his country and was willing to go back to fight for it. I love it, too, and I loved him with great pride for the bravery that was still a part of him. He was never more special than at that moment.

Trials and tribulations over weekend discomforts and dissonance continued, but never again with the same impact I had felt before September 11. Sadness, depression and loss that moved from a personal arena to a global scale of destruction and horror changed my perspective. Alzheimer's rejoiced in teaching me that life, love and courage can transcend personal circumstances in the face of universal tragedy.

My prayer of gratitude for Michael and for the moments we had finally shared continued, too, although I held on to the right to say at the start of each week a fervent "Thank Goodness it's Monday."

There are some things, as you learn to live with Alzheimer's, which are entirely understandable.

WHEN THE TIME COMES

The heartache of facility placement

Eleven

When the Time Comes

It was the week of Thanksgiving, a warm and sunny North Carolina day, when the phone rang in my kitchen.

"Mrs. Ellis? This is Ellen Smith at the NC State Veterans Nursing Home in Fayetteville. I'm calling to tell you that we have a placement opening for Mr. Ellis."

My thoughts and my heart froze, refusing to understand. Michael's name had been on the waiting list for several months, all the paperwork in order except for final signatures, but it was filed neatly in the back of my mind. I couldn't seem to make sense of these words while I was busy putting away groceries for Thanksgiving meals; recipes and anticipation of company all I was thinking about.

"What does this mean?" I asked in a voice that didn't sound like mine at all.

The answer came matter-of-factly. "It means that we need to choose a date for you to bring him, if you still want to place him with us," was the quiet response from Lieutenant Colonel Smith.

"Do you mean now?" I stammered.

"Yes, but we can take into consideration the Thanksgiving holiday and allow a little leeway in your arrival. We can't keep the opening long, but we can adjust the timeline due to the holiday."

Again, my thoughts seemed to be unable to grasp what was happening. Now? How could this be happening now? Did this mean that I was actually facing taking my husband to live there *now*?

I had visited every nursing home in the area during the year, telling myself that it would be a long time before I needed one for Michael. Visiting these places before I actually needed a placement was the only way I could handle the emotions. I learned a lot, including that there was nothing I could afford and also that visible amenities did not guarantee quality of care. I subsequently went to the local Veterans Administration office to see what financial aid might be possible, since Michael had served in the Air Force in World War II. Aid was available; I visited and admired the new Veterans Nursing Home facility in Fayetteville, and I had committed to their waiting list a few months prior. I was told that the waiting list could be up to a year long, so there had been no need for me to worry that I would be placing Michael any time soon. All of a sudden, with the telephone heavy in my hand, the words heavy in my heart, the "now" was here. The time had come.

"Would you let me call you on Monday after Thanksgiving to set a date?" I asked tentatively, as my brain returned to the phone call.

Colonel Smith's reply of, "That will be fine. Please remember that we need to admit him within a few days. I'll wait for you to call next Monday with your decision," allowed my breath to return so that at least my heart started beating again.

Hanging up the phone, I moved as though in a dream to sit in a chair at the table. I had taken the afternoon off from work to shop, something I had to do before picking Michael up from his adult day center later in the day. I had been filling the pantry with things to create a happy holiday experience, which suddenly had no meaning at all. I looked at the clock, thinking simultaneously that I didn't know how to face him. *How could I look at the face I loved and know that I was going to make him go to a place to live without me? What if he sensed that I was plotting something behind his back? Would he somehow be able to tell that I was sending him away? Would he think that I didn't want him anymore? How and what would I tell him when the time came?*

I picked up the phone and dialed. "Judy," I said to the director of his day center, "I've had a call from the Veterans Home," and began to sob. "They have an opening for Michael. I have to call next Monday and let them know when I'm bringing him. How can I *do* this? How can I give him away like this?"

"Come on down here now, so we can talk a few minutes before you see Michael to pick him up. I'll meet you at the lobby door."

Her voice was calm. Mine was anything but. I don't remember the drive to the center. Her arms encircled me as I stumbled into the building, and she just held me as I cried and tried desperately to breathe. Guiding me to a private room, she sat with me and held my hands. Judy had gone with me to visit the Fayetteville facility on two occasions months before, to help me determine the quality and suitability of it for Michael.

"First of all, you are not giving him away. You are letting him go to a fine place where they will know how to take care of him and you will have the chance to be with him as often as you like. You can live without depleting your health any further. You will have the opportunity to recover your strength, so that you will be here for him as long as he needs you. You are not giving him away; you are giving yourself what is necessary to survive the ordeal of caregiving."

I looked at her blankly, her face swimming before me through my tears, trying desperately to understand her words. I was exhausted and depressed. I was sleep-deprived and constantly on alert to make instantaneous choices for the daily challenges that confronted me. My head knew the reality of my waning energy, but this was the moment when my heart was doing the thinking. My heart wanted me to cling to him and had never been less concerned with myself; it was pounding with the words *How can I do this to him?* I wasn't the one who mattered. He was my only concern. Judy, with her wisdom and experience, made me look at the fact that I had to have myself as a concern, too. Sitting with her, gripping her hands like a lifeline, her calm words put my situation in a perspective that gave me, at least, a partial understanding of the danger of trying to continue as we were. I saw the specter of the sleepless nights, his paranoid thoughts and fears, the management of even small daily details; and I felt the exhaustion of these past few years wash over me. It was time, as she said, to try to regain some of my strength. It was time to ensure his care without the hands-on daily responsibility part of it. The word "time" seemed to course through my veins, finally making its way to my brain. The time had come.

During the days that followed, as the thought occurred to me that nothing had to happen before Thanksgiving, I began thinking that maybe I could put off placement until after Christmas. That wouldn't be too much to ask, surely. If they weren't going to make me bring him before Thanksgiving, they couldn't possibly expect me to bring him before Christmas. That was just too soon. Ellen Smith was a caring, compassionate person; of course she would grant my request to wait until after Christmas. I began planning my plea.

The only thing I remember clearly that Thanksgiving was the grief, pain and guilt. Not the food, decorations, or family. I was acutely aware every second of every waking moment that this would be the last Thanksgiving Michael would ever spend at home with me. I functioned in a fog of wrenching disbelief. I cried myself silently to sleep every night, wracked with guilt and missing him as if he had already gone. My misery was so intense that I began to wonder how much longer I could stand it. I had moments, honestly, of feeling as though I were sinking out of sight, into an abyss from which I would never emerge. I began to see that I was at a breaking point and knew that I could not go through this for Christmas, too. It would not be possible to survive this last Thanksgiving and live through our last Christmas here, too. I had to make this move before Christmas. I could not plead for more time and more agony.

Talking with my son Matt and my sisters restored some of my equanimity, since they voiced their support of the placement decision as had Judy. They, also, pointed out the chance for me to regain my strength, to be able to function in Michael's best interest, with him and for him. Matt and I planned the date for placement so that he could come from Minneapolis to help me.

The last part of the plan was when I called Judy and asked "Would it be possible for you to go with Matt and me to take Michael to the Veterans Home?"

Her immediate response was, "Of course. I've been planning to all along, if you wanted me."

The hardest phone call I ever made was to Lieutenant Colonel Smith, the Monday after Thanksgiving, to confirm Michael's arrival for the second week in December. There was an acrid taste in my mouth, limited space in my lungs for air, and I seemed to have no bones in my legs to stand to make that call from our kitchen wall phone. After I hung up, I pushed my mind immediately to the list of things a family had to prepare: clothing and personal items necessary for the person who was going there to live. It was a surreal flashback to getting Matt's things ready for him to go to summer camp when he was a child. I wouldn't let myself dwell on the difference. There was a strange comfort about doing what I had done then, for the best and happiest of reasons. I clung to that unrealistic familiarity; and as bizarre as it was, make no apology for letting it carry me through the preparations for Michael's move.

Matt arrived two days before we took Michael to Fayetteville. We had planned that the two of us, with Judy, would have a private talk with Michael at the day care center before the end of the next day. Judy took us all to a private room, and I began my "announcement." I told them that I had agreed to do some traveling for my job, and since that meant that I would not be home as usual, I had found a place for Michael to stay while I was out of town. It was a place where other veterans from the Air Force stayed when their families were not at home and that I liked it very much. I heard the words come out of my mouth as though I were reading from a book that couldn't possibly belong to me. I didn't elaborate much; just enough so that Michael got the idea that he was going someplace other than home. Judy and Matt talked about how nice it would be for Michael to have company when I was off traveling. Michael made a couple of comments about being fine at home, but none of us responded or contradicted him.

He remained silent after that but finally looked at me and said, "I'm proud of you for your new job."

That touched me deeply, and hurt just as deeply. I didn't have a new job; I had the new heart-wrenching trial of taking Michael to live in a place without me. I knew that it wasn't exactly clear to him what was happening, but it was my way of giving him some idea that he was going to be visiting a different place. Nothing more was said about it when we got home.

After Michael went to bed that night, Matt put the suitcase in the car. I didn't watch. I was clinging to my last vestige of control. I laid down beside Michael in bed for the last time. When I closed my eyes that night it was only in prayer, not in sleep. I was praying for forgiveness.

The next morning, I selected Michael's favorite sweater, slacks and sport coat to wear and thought with satisfaction how handsome he looked. Once in the car, as Matt backed out of our driveway I couldn't look at the house. It would be there when we returned, but it would never see Michael enter its door again. I was numb and cold, holding on rigidly to suppress my emotions. We met Judy at the front of the day care center and Matt drove us to Fayetteville. Michael was in front with Matt, and Judy and I were in the back seat. She squeezed my hand from time to time, conveying her strength and reassurance to me with her touch. She and Matt were wonderful at keeping conversation going, with only occasional sentences or responses from me. Michael appeared to be unaware of the reason for our ride and was calm and relaxed. Once in Fayetteville, we went to a restaurant for lunch, which pleased Michael very much. He had always loved eating out, and this was a special treat. I had difficulty swallowing food, since my heart seemed to have lodged in my throat and taken up all the space reserved for that function. My hand shook so visibly when trying to hold my glass of tea that I didn't attempt it again after the first try.

When lunch was finished, we continued on to the Veterans Home. I had a momentary panic when we turned into the drive where the sign proclaimed the "NC State Veterans Nursing Home," in letters far larger than I had remembered. Huge letters that might as well have been in neon lights. I couldn't imagine how I could have forgotten how big that sign was and cringed in the back seat for fear of Michael's reaction on seeing it. He didn't see it, or couldn't read it, or some miracle occurred that kept him from noticing it. When Matt stopped the car in the circle drive in front of the beautiful porch, Michael announced that he was going to wait for us in the car.

Matt just said, simply but firmly, "We're all going in to see this place, Mike. Come on." As Judy and I exited the back seat, Michael opened the car door and got out. Matt linked his arm through Michael's and started talking about something as we walked through the automatic door.

Lieutenant Colonel Smith was in the lobby, came to Michael with her hand outstretched and said, "Mr. Ellis, how pleased I am to meet you. I've been looking forward to showing you something we are very proud of for our veterans."

The social side of Michael took over as he smiled at her and said, "I'm glad to see you, too."

We proceeded down the wide hallway with its gleaming floor, stopped to admire the small aviary with brightly-colored small birds fluttering around, and turned right to continue to a set of closed doors. Again I panicked, knowing those doors only opened when a code was punched into a keypad and thinking that Michael might become alarmed at the obvious security. He had no reaction to that process, since Colonel Smith kept up a running commentary about the birds we had just seen being a wonderful gift, as she deftly entered the numbers.

Once inside, we saw men of various ages walking around, some talking in small groups, some sitting in wheel chairs, and women in colorful smocks talking and busily interacting with the men. Colonel Smith took us past the large center of activity to a room on the left, fitted out with two beds, two dressers, two small closets, and a big window looking out onto a nicely manicured lawn.

She said to Michael, "Mr. Ellis, while you are staying here, we'll put your name in this place beside the door so everyone will know where you are."

He smiled, examined the place where a name card would fit and moved back out into the hall to the reception area. I could not think of one word to say, was shaking with panic and feeling tears just behind my eyes, and was truly grateful when one of the women dressed in a smock was introduced to us.

She told Michael how handsome he looked and suggested, "I'd like you to meet some of my friends." She linked her arm with his and steered him over to a small alcove area where three more women in smocks were standing around a scale.

"I bet we can guess your weight, Mr. Ellis," one of them said and began helping him to step up on the scale.

They gathered around Michael, laughing and guessing his weight, and he was totally focused on their attention. Colonel Smith motioned for us to step away and quietly opened the secure doors for us to leave. In shock, I stepped through the doors, they closed, and I knew it was over. He was inside, I was outside; there had been no hug or kiss or good-bye. I crumpled onto Matt's chest as Judy walked on down the hall fighting her own emotions, and I went to pieces. All of a sudden, there was nothing else to do.

I remember feeling a hand on my shoulder and a man's voice saying "I promise we'll take good care of him. We care about all our veterans." Later I learned that it was the doctor assigned to Michael's wing, and I was comforted at the thought that he knew how frightened for Michael I was. And for myself. And for Michael's life, and for mine.

We finally walked to the lobby and I just stood there while Matt brought Michael's suitcase into Colonel Smith's office. The only thing to do now was to go home. Home without Michael. The time had come and it was now. I had survived living with Alzheimer's at home; my new challenge would be to survive living with it as a visitor. I would do it.

CHAPTER TWELVE

MICHAEL'S PLACE

Visiting after placement

Twelve

Michael's Place

How was it possible that I had slept all night? It was the first night I had spent at home without Michael since he had been placed in the NC State Veterans Nursing Home. My son Matt and I, along with our friend Judy, the director of Michael's adult day care center, had taken him on the one-hour and twenty-minute drive to Fayetteville yesterday. When we left there, we knew Michael would never come home again. That night, numb and still not believing it, once I had fallen asleep, I had slept until daylight. Exhaustion and guilt had taken its toll on my mind and body. Knowing that, however, did not ease the heavy sense of loss and grief I felt when I awakened. Stumbling downstairs to make coffee, I also made enough noise that Matt followed me down almost immediately.

He put his arms around me and asked, "Are you alright, Mom?"

Through yet more tears, I answered, "No, I'm not. I'm shaking and guilty and I don't know how I could have done this. I'm not sure I can live with it. What if something happens to him and I'm not there?"

Matt just held me and didn't reply. There was nothing he could have said that would ease my distress.

After regaining some control, made possible by the simple, normal act of pouring coffee and sitting at the dining room table, I blurted out, "I don't want to sleep in our bed anymore. I don't want to sleep in our bedroom, even."

"Whatever you want, we'll make happen," was Matt's calm and decisive answer. I already knew what I wanted: it was a major rearrangement of the downstairs.

I hesitated before telling him, rather sheepishly, "I want to convert the office into the dining room and I want the daybed from the office moved into here." That meant disassembling everything in order to move furniture through the doorways, and it would be a huge job.

"Sounds like a plan to me," Matt replied with a smile on his face.

Bless him. Smiling at what, to me, seemed an onerous task was something I hadn't expected. Where was the once teen-ager who would have said, "Oh, Mom! Do we have to?" complete with rolling his eyes heavenward and heavy sighing.

That young man had become a mature adult during the years of living in other states, and I hadn't had the time or opportunity to notice, I guess. There was only love and support in his being part of this life-changing event for me, helping in ways that conveyed his willingness to do whatever he could do for me. My guilty feeling about wanting him to move furniture instead of calling or seeing his friends slid to the back of my mind as we started the process.

It took most of the day, taking apart the dining room table and propping it in the kitchen while he took the daybed apart, and together we moved the framework into the dining room. Rearranging other pieces of furniture was difficult, too. I had to unload the small buffet in order to move it into the new dining area, and we had to move the desk that held the computer and all those pieces that go with it to another place in the office. Finally, everything was re-assembled in the new spaces. The daybed, in what I would now call the sitting room, was placed so that I could lie there and look out into the back yard, watching the birdfeeders that hosted many and varied winged friends, even now in the month of December. I could anticipate early mornings listening to bird songs and picture the summer flowers that would be planted in the spring. We made one other change, which was to move Michael's favorite chair to a different place in the living room.

Within the next few days, I realized that I didn't like sitting at the dining room table, now in a small room with the desk, computer, bookcase and buffet. It looked out onto the front yard of our townhouse, at the driveway and walkway that would never see Michael arriving home again. Instead, I put a small rocking chair and folding tray at the end of the daybed in front of the sliding glass patio door, and that became my morning coffee table as well as the main place I would sit any time during the day or evening. Evening meals I ate sometimes on another folding tray in the living room, a habit Michael and I had developed when it was easier to watch television while we ate supper than try to converse. I hadn't liked that either, but then living with Alzheimer's creates the need to be adaptable, among many other things.

Matt had to return to Minneapolis the day after we finished converting the two rooms. I dropped him off at the airport, giving him a brief hug and pulling away from the curb quickly, incapable of saying "good-bye." Tears and intense emotion were playing havoc with my ability to drive. I only went the brief distance to the Observation Deck parking lot at Raleigh-Durham Airport and stopped, giving myself time to cry. I was blessed with this special person who had become much more than a cherished little boy; now a capable, caring best friend. I knew him now in a different way: not just as the child who had inspired deep love, appreciation and pride, but also as a dependable adult whose love was returned with the capacity to awaken within me the knowledge that I had been given a gift from God on the day he was born.

Life was, and still is in a misty memory, at a stand-still for the next eighteen days. The Veterans Administration officer at the nursing home had advised me at the time of application that families were asked not to visit after placement for a minimum of two weeks, preferably longer, in order for the patient to become adjusted. Because of my career in taking children with disabilities into the small school that I directed, even though it was not a residential school, I knew how much better it was on the children not to have their parents visible during the initial days of school. I knew that seeing me each day in the beginning of Michael's move to the Veterans Home would be confusing to him. Even though he no longer knew my name or that I was his wife, his response to me always indicated that he recognized me as somebody familiar. I also felt certain that I would be unable to deal with his wanting to leave with me, if he thought he should. Matt was planning to return to go with me on my first visit at the end of the waiting period. It would be Christmas Day. I had to wait, and it was unbearably hard. I had taken the first days of Michael's placement off from work, and then the school where I was the Principal would be closed until January.

During those days of waiting, I rarely moved from that rocking chair in front of the patio door, except occasionally to shower and put on comfortable sweat pants and shirt. I watched the clock each morning until nine o'clock, when I could call the nursing home. Calling was not enough, but I was determined to make Michael's adjustment as successful as it could be by staying away.

"Good morning, Michelle," I said that first phone call, in a timidly fearful voice to the head nurse assigned to Michael. "How is he?"

"Mr. Ellis is doing just fine," she replied. Her voice was much more assured than mine. "He is so polite! He thanks us for anything we do for him and we're not used to that very much, I can tell you!" she volunteered enthusiastically. Visions in my mind of his moping around in crushing depression dissolved a little.

"Right now he's getting a manicure from one of our student nurses and I can hear them laughing and talking. She's enjoying his company, and he loves the attention. The night nurse told me this morning that she discovered him awake last night, and they had an ice cream party."

"Did you say ice cream party?" I asked in surprise.

"Yes, she took him into the nurses' break room, and they had a bowl of ice cream together. He loved it and went back to bed afterward and slept the rest of the night."

My gratitude knew no bounds. Ice cream was a favorite of his and he would have loved anybody who gave him some. I loved her, too, sight unseen. He was obviously being treated like a special guest instead of a hospital patient. I hung up the phone, put my head back as I sat in the rocking chair, and slept.

Thank goodness Matt came back to drive us to Fayetteville to see Michael for my first visit. I was so nervous that it would have been all but dangerous for me to try to drive it alone. I had prepared some small Christmas decorations for his room and had managed to bake some cookies for him and the nursing staff. I knew from experience that I couldn't take a present, because he would be upset if he didn't have anything for us if Matt and I gave him anything that looked like a gift. As we parked in the Nursing Home lot, I had to take a few moments to compose myself and find something resembling a smile inside myself instead of the tears that were threatening to burst forth. While my heart wanted to rush headlong to him, my legs felt like heavy wooden logs attached to a weak, shaky body. My guilty conscience was prodding me to expect the worst, which was evident in the bitter taste of bile in my mouth.

We walked into the locked unit, using the door code that the receptionist had handed me, and saw Michael sitting in the main area around the large curved nurses' desk.

"Hi, honey. I'm so glad to see you," was all I could manage to say, as I leaned down to kiss him on the cheek. The fragrance of shampoo and talcum powder wafted gently from him. He looked at me, smiled, and stood up. He hugged me rather tentatively, grinned at Matt and hugged him, too. At least we were friends. At least that.

I said a quick, silent *Thank you, God.*

Somewhere deep in my heart I had been terrified that he would take one look at me and say, "Why did you leave me in this place? Where have you been? Are you taking me home now?"

Thank you, God. Just maybe the torture of not visiting him for eighteen days had been worth it.

"Let me show you something," he said before we sat down. He led us straight to his room door and pointed to the name-card holder on the frame. "This is my name. They know who I am," he said proudly.

Matt and I crowded around him to peer at it closely, and Matt said, "Of course they know who you are, buddy," clapping Michael on the shoulder.

We entered the room and Michael said, in a hushed voice, "Look at this." Walking to the head of his bed, he reached for the light pull-string and glanced around as if to see if anyone else were watching. He pulled it once and one light turned on; again and a different light came on; and with the third pull, both lights came on.

"Have you ever seen anything like this? It's wonderful," he added, again in a voice that indicated he was probably the only one who had such a magic light and he didn't want anybody else to know about it.

When I had called several days before to tell them we would be visiting that day, we were told we could have lunch with Michael in the dining room. We proceeded there and found his table. We all sat and watched while two women entered, pushing and pulling a large, stainless steel shelf-device on wheels, loaded with food trays. While they were distributed, Matt and I introduced ourselves to the other men at the table and met the man who shared Michael's room. I couldn't call him a roommate, because they both had Alzheimer's and didn't know each other's names or have conversational skills. His name was Walter, and I had noticed a picture of a family group on Walter's dresser in their room. I later learned that Walter's family had moved to another state and had stopped visiting him a long time ago, but that he didn't seem to remember and never asked about them. I tried each time I visited to be especially friendly to Walter, but he had no interest in me whatsoever, so nothing like recognition or a friendship ever happened.

When lunch was over, I noticed that Michael was getting less and less animated and seemed very tired. It was, I took note, the time of day when residents were drifting on their own, or being escorted, to their respective rooms to rest. It was suddenly time to leave, and I had not thought about that part of the visit. My mind had been totally consumed with getting there and seeing him, not with leaving him again. My stomach muscles clenched involuntarily as panic rose in my breast. I had arranged the small decorations on Michael's dresser, but he didn't seem to know what they were or why I had put them there. The most I can say for that effort was that *I* knew they were there, and maybe the staff would get the idea that someone still loved and cared about Michael, not like Walter.

I was leaving him again, and again I didn't know how to do it. He stood with us at the door to his room and Matt started the departure by hugging Michael and saying something I didn't take in. At least I understood that Michael didn't seem to think he was supposed to go with us.

"I'll see you again soon, honey," I said as I gave him a hug.

Out of the corner of my eye, I had noticed a nurse standing by the door keypad, so we walked through the doors as they opened without having to stop and punch the numbers. I hadn't trusted myself to look back. The clean fragrance that enveloped him, and gratitude that he didn't hate me, had filled my senses and heart and stayed with me as we crossed the threshold. I also carried out of there the sound of the pleasant voices of the nurses as they had gone about their duties, especially serving lunches and helping several residents with eating. They had joked and laughed, teasing each other and some of the patients, in an atmosphere of good humor. Those were comforting images that I clung to on our way home, as well as knowing that I could go back tomorrow and any time as often as I liked from then on.

I repeated silently, *Forgive me, God* several times as we walked to the front lobby.

But I also said "Thank you, God" out loud and to myself, as Matt drove us back to Raleigh. I was still living with Alzheimer's but from now on it would be as a visitor to Michael's place.

CHAPTER THIRTEEN

AND THE BIRDS SANG

Peace at the end

Thirteen

And the Birds Sang

My daybed was comfortable; I lay there in the early morning light, unwilling to move, keeping my eyes closed but not sleeping. The voice on the answering machine kept repeating in my head on a "continuous play" setting, as it had for over a week.

"Mrs. Ellis, this is Estelle Williams at the Veterans Home. Please call immediately when you get this message. It's an emergency."

During the ten months that my husband Michael had been a resident in the Veterans Home, he had been taken by ambulance to the local hospital three times: once when he had multiple seizures and twice with double pneumonia. Was this one of those emergencies again?

I had caught her voice on the answering machine as I came in the door but had grabbed the phone too late. Lying there on this clear, quiet morning I remembered, yet again, dialing the number from memory hurriedly, unable to breathe, hoping I could talk. Ms. Williams was the head nurse in a different wing of the nursing home, where Michael had been placed after his last stay in the hospital. He had only been in that new wing four days; his bed in the familiar wing had been taken by someone else while he was hospitalized.

The scene in my mind continued. My son Matt, home because Michael had been so seriously ill, had been helping me put my suitcase in the car and had followed me in the door that morning. He stood there watching my face anxiously as I dialed the Nursing Home. When I was connected with Ms. Williams, I pictured her neat, matronly figure and pretty silver hair as I heard her voice.

"Mrs. Ellis, there is no easy way to tell you this. I put Mr. Ellis in the wheelchair and rolled him out to the nurses' station this morning, so I could talk to him as I worked while we waited for you to come. I spoke to him each time I passed while I was delivering medications and then I noticed that he was drooling. I stopped to wipe his mouth and I realized that he was gone."

Gone where? My mind had pictured his getting up and walking out of sight. My thoughts had leaped ahead: he couldn't walk anymore. He couldn't stand up. Or talk. And then it hit me. *No. Not that.*

"Are you telling me he has *died? Has he died?*" I repeated, close to hysterics. My eyes flew to Matt, seeing him trying to control the look on his face, and I knew mine was registering horror.

"I'm so sorry, Mrs. Ellis. Can I call someone to come be with you?" she had asked quietly after a brief pause.

"No, no, my son is here," I said to her in what little voice I had; then to Matt, "Michael has died. He has *died.*" My voice was very loud by this time, in disbelief. The words seemed to be words I had never heard before. Strange words that could not possibly mean what they implied. No. I was supposed to be with him. I was supposed to be holding his hand. I was supposed to be beside him. This couldn't be happening. I had just left there yesterday evening, after Ms. Williams and I had discussed how much stronger and more alert Michael had seemed all day.

"Do you think I could slip away and go home to do laundry and come back in the morning?" I had asked, feeling encouraged that Michael appeared much better than he had in three days. I had been staying for more than a week in a guest house that was for families of hospital and nursing home patients. "My son is coming in from Minneapolis tonight and I could meet him and come back tomorrow, if you think it's safe for me to leave." She had agreed, saying that now was probably the best time to go. I liked her. She was calm and kind, with a reassuring manner clearly showing that she had been nursing for many years. So I had left there, knowing that once I returned to Fayetteville the following day I would not leave again, because I had been told Michael did not have much longer. I had driven back to Raleigh, planning to be certain I would return with enough clothes to last for as many days as I would need them. Matt and I had been preparing to go that next morning when Ms. Williams had called.

The memories crowded in as I still lay in my daybed on this morning. Like watching a movie, I saw in my mind that I had been clutching the telephone while hearing the dreaded news, feeling suddenly dizzy, and said to Ms. Williams, "Here's my son," thrusting the phone at Matt. I had been unable to think and knew I had to sit down.

I heard Matt say, "We're ready to leave. We'll be there as soon as Mom can make it. What do we need to do?"

When I heard Matt say those words, I had jumped up, saying frantically, "I have to call Duke. I have to call Duke. I'm supposed to call them as soon as Michael dies . . . . I have to call."

Ms. Williams obviously heard my voice, because the next thing I heard Matt say was, "Thank you. I'll tell Mom and we'll be on the way."

"Ms. Williams has already called Duke, Mom. She knew the procedure and it's all been taken care of.

He put his arms around me then and said, "You don't have to go down there, Mom. I can go. You don't have to go."

"Oh, yes, I have to go. I have to get to him. I have to see him. I have to go," was my answer. I grabbed my pocketbook and headed out the door. Matt followed.

The urgency I had felt about calling Duke was because I had been given permission to donate Michael's brain to the Alzheimer's Research Center at Duke University Hospital. Having learned about this possibility more than a year before, I had gone through a lengthy procedure to be accepted into the donation program. Michael and I had always agreed that we would be organ donors and I knew he would want to do this. If we could save just one other family from suffering through Alzheimer's disease, it was the right thing to do. The nursing home had been given all the instructions that required immediate steps at the time of death, and it was those instructions that had flooded into my consciousness when Matt was speaking to Ms. Williams on the phone.

Once Matt had turned the car in the direction of Fayetteville, my cell phone rang, the first of two calls I would receive on the way. I had been told that I would be called twice as soon as Duke was informed of the death.

Each call was to be sure that I could, in fact, continue with the brain donation plan. I would be asked twice and the calls would be recorded. The research program did not want anyone regretting their permission, which sometimes happened when the death of the loved one actually occurred. The first call was a shock, since the caller put into words that Michael had died. Whoever the man was, he expressed his sympathy before reminding me that they were required to ask if I were sure I wanted to follow through with the donation procedure. When I managed to say yes, not doubting the decision at all, he again reminded me that I would receive another call within half an hour for the same reason. That call came and I reiterated my permission. That meant that they would send an ambulance from Duke to pick up Michael's body within two hours. Still lost in this memory, I recall that Matt was parking the car in the Veterans Home parking lot before I even realized where we were. I had rushed inside, feeling a panic as though I needed to get to Michael before something happened . . . as though he were not gone yet.

★   ★   ★

I opened my eyes and pushed the vivid memories aside. I was alone in the house, all my family and Matt having left, and it was quiet. I moved in slow motion through taking a shower and putting on my clothes. Finally sitting in the rocking chair with my coffee, looking at the bird feeders,

I saw only a lone male cardinal, without his mate and he wasn't singing. I blinked and he was gone. I couldn't see anything else. My eyes seemed to have a film over them, showing only the images of that day of loss, when Michael had died without my being there. Reflected in that film, I saw clearly how Matt and I had walked down the hallway in the nursing home and saw Ms. Williams standing there. She hugged us both gently. She took us to the doorway of the room where Michael was laid on the bed and stayed discreetly just outside the door. My first thought as I saw him was how peaceful he looked. There was no stress, no suffering, no pain on his face. He was dressed in one of his favorite knit shirts and navy blue slacks, lying comfortably with a soft blanket covering his feet. It was September 27, just two weeks before his eighty-fourth birthday. His hair was neatly combed, his face shaven, and he looked rested. As I leaned over and kissed him on the cheek, stroking his forehead and taking his hand in mine, I became aware of a noise behind me. I turned to see Matt crying, struggling for silence, with tears streaming down his face. I put my arms around him and we stood there, both sobbing our grief and trying to console each other. I remember that I turned to Ms. Williams and thanked her for her care of Michael and for making sure that he looked so handsome. I was profoundly thankful that I had seen him in this peaceful state, relieved of all the stress of struggling with even the smallest details of living. He was at rest. His journey through the ravages of Alzheimer's was over.

When we were finally ready to leave that room, I told Ms. Williams that I didn't want to take any of Michael's clothes or personal items and to please give them to anyone there who needed them. I had already taken the photos home when Michael had been hospitalized. There was nothing else I wanted.

The scene being played in my mind on this particular morning moved ahead then, recalling my asking Ms. Williams if Michelle, the head nurse in Michael's previous wing, might possibly be there. When Ms. Williams told me that she was, I asked if she would call Michelle to meet me in the hall, because I wanted to thank her and tell her good-bye. I knew I couldn't go into that wing, but I couldn't leave without seeing her. Ms. Williams picked up the house phone as Matt and I walked to the hallway leading to the other wing. As we approached the locked doors, they opened. Out came Michelle, along with every other nurse that had ever been assigned to assist in Michael's care.

Matt said later, to family and friends, "Those doors opened and a wave of humanity walked out. It was amazing. It was obvious they loved Mike, and they loved Mom, too."

I had started crying and so did they. They each hugged me in turn. I thanked them as best I could, and Matt took me by the hand to lead me away, to make our final trip from Fayetteville back to Raleigh.

*   *   *

My rocking chair was still, and my coffee was cold. I had fallen asleep again, as I seemed to do often. The memories of that last day in Fayetteville faded for the moment and I was conscious of an overwhelming fatigue. There was no energy in my body; only an ache that engulfed my heart and made it difficult to swallow. There seemed to be no room for anything but the grief. I later learned that my adrenal glands had shut down, after having driven my body and mind for ten years. They had quit supplying me with the fuel that had been necessary to keep me functioning in that over-alert mode that had become my normal state of being. They recovered eventually, as did I, but it took many months. It has taken much longer than that to be able to tell this story.

As time passed, other memories of our ten months in the Veterans Home began to take precedence over the nightmare of the day Michael died. During the first month of his residence, he told me confidentially one day that Walter, the man who shared his room, was the sheriff and to steer clear of him. Walter could sometimes be demanding and raise his voice, although I never saw anything that would have explained this behavior. The very next day when I visited, Michael thought Walter worked for him and had evidently decided not to be the sheriff anymore.

I had watched that day as Michael removed the daily schedule that was on the bulletin board, then followed him as he found Walter in the dining room and said to him, much to my surprise, "Could you go make a copy of this as soon as you have time?"

The amusing part was that Walter must also have thought Michael was the boss, at least for the moment, because he took the schedule and said, "Yes, sir. I'll get right to it."

I distracted Michael at that moment, not sure how this would play out. Walter walked away with the schedule, and the entire incident was forgotten by both of them immediately. Walter was in and out of the room numerous times after that but he never so much as glanced at us and we never saw either the copy or the original schedule again.

I still smile, too, at the way Michael never remembered that the walker they gave him was his to use, even though it had his name on it. I would arrive to visit, find him sitting in a chair in the area near the nurses' desk and have to find his walker before we could go to one of the parlors or out into the fenced back yard. There was an elderly, dark-skinned man in a wheelchair, usually sitting in the vicinity, who was the main source of information for the nurses.

Whenever something was missing, someone would invariably say, "Mr. Collins, did you see what happened to . . . (whatever it was)?"

He would smile and answer, in his quiet, deep voice, "Yes. It got put over there behind that sofa." I finally learned to turn to Mr. Collins, too, instead of stopping a busy nurse, to ask if he knew where Michael's walker was.

He always did and told me one day, chuckling, "He likes to stick it behind the piano." Bless Mr. Collins. He kept that wing of the nursing home running as smoothly as it could. Other times, when the walker was beside Michael while we were sitting there for our visit, Michael would stop anyone who happened to walk by, push the walker out in front of him and say, "Hey, is this yours?"

And sometimes the person asked would say, "Yes, that's mine," and walk away carrying the walker with him. I'd follow discreetly until it was abandoned and bring it back to Michael.

Lunch or dinner time at the Veterans Home was always interesting. There was more activity and more interaction among the residents, and between them and the staff. On one of my first visits there, we were sitting at one of the dining room tables waiting for lunch. A nurses' assistant whom I had not yet met stopped beside Michael, who was sitting at the end of the long table.

"Hi, Mr. Ellis," she said in a friendly voice, "I wanted to let you know that I'm back from vacation. Is this your wife?"

Michael quickly turned his head in my direction, with a questioning look on his face. I nodded. "Yes," he said back to her.

She asked, "What is her name?" as though prompting him to introduce us.

With no hesitation, Michael leaned over to me and said quietly, "What do you like to be called?"

I leaned toward him and answered, quietly, too, "I like to be called Martha-Lee."

He sat back, looked at the nurse and spoke in a confident voice, "She likes to be called Martha-Lee."

The nurse and I smiled at each other before she walked away, although my smile was much broader than hers. I couldn't tell if she didn't know him well enough yet to realize he wouldn't know the answer to either of those questions, but Michael had handled a potentially embarrassing situation with great social skill. I thought it was wonderful for him to have thought of just the right way to find out who I was. It was pretty brilliant, really. I felt like a proud Mama!

Weight loss, and sometimes gain, is always a concern for nursing home patients and mealtimes gave me a chance to see how much Michael ate. I had noticed a couple of times that he didn't know which utensil to use and he always ate dessert first, but I was satisfied with his appetite for a while. One Sunday we were having baked chicken, which I cut into pieces for him, mashed potatoes with gravy, and garden peas. I watched in some trepidation as Michael picked up his knife and began using his fingers to scoop peas onto it. Before I could do anything, he guided that knife, filled with garden peas, to his mouth, never dropping a single one. I was amazed. I could never have done that if I tried a hundred times. It was truly impressive.

After Michael was confined to a wheelchair, sometimes I would push him onto the beautiful, spacious front porch where I could sit in a rocking chair beside him so we could enjoy the sunshine and fresh air together. Michael loved looking at the flags overhead that waved proudly in the breeze: the American flag, the NC State flag, and the dramatic Missing in Action flag of the armed forces.

To vary our routine, we would sometimes sit on the small patio or in the back yard outside the main television parlor. The yard was a very large parcel of land neatly landscaped and handsomely fenced. The far side was a very high steep hill, straight as a cliff, which would have made even a mountain goat abandon any attempt to negotiate it.

Michael had very little language left, so conversation was less than satisfying and scenery was important to our sense of enjoyment. He could say some words and some familiar phrases, but he couldn't put thought processes into meaningful sentences. While sitting outside on the patio one warm afternoon, Michael began trying to talk. He gestured to the hill, said some words about trucks and continued talking in non-words, mixed with an occasional real word, and becoming very animated. I watched him in fascination, totally unable to understand anything he was saying, but I perfectly understood that he was excited. I began to smile, and as he watched me, laughter took over. He leaned back in the chair, laughing with me, and then leaned forward to pat me on the knee. We were both laughing hard, and his eyes were watching my face intently. When our mirth subsided, he drew a deep breath and started all over again. Same gestures, same sounds and words, and I knew he was trying to repeat the funny story he had just told. It was a marvelous moment of laughter, which was reminiscent and typical of our former life together. It felt wonderful, and I believe in the deepest part of my heart that Michael recognized it, too, as part of who we used to be. It was like sitting on the edge of time. I shall never forget how golden that moment felt, when we suddenly shared happiness. It never happened again, but that memory refuses to be stuck in with the ones labeled "sad." It was simply happy, and the contentment remains one of my memories to savor.

Yes, there were times when being at the Veterans Home felt good. I never went there that I didn't take a box of Dunkin' Donuts doughnut holes to the nursing and cleaning staff. I'd pick out one for Michael and one for me before laying it on the nurses' station desk. I was particularly pleased one day when I left the box at the desk while no one was sitting there, and later heard someone proclaim, "Mrs. Ellis must be here; I see the doughnuts!"

It was my gesture of gratitude for all of them, in recognition of their many kindnesses to Michael of which I was often aware.

When he could still talk in meaningful words, sometimes he would walk up to the desk and say, "Have you heard from my ride yet? I'm being transferred, you know."

Invariably, regardless of the person on duty, the reply was a kind response, "No, sir, they haven't called yet. We'll let you know just as soon as we hear from them."

That was all that was necessary. No explaining that there was no transfer, no ride coming; the things so many people don't know to avoid. They were always, without exception, kind and positive.

One other memory that always makes me smile is the actual incident that sounds like an old joke about memory loss. I had excused myself to go to the ladies room and when I returned to my seat beside Michael in the parlor, he looked at me and said, "There was a woman here just a while ago who had on a dress just like yours."

Yes, it really happened. No joke. At home later, sitting alone in the rocking chair by the door and watching the birds on the feeder, I wished I could tell them about it. But they flew away, and they still didn't sing.

These are the memories that I keep in my heart, just as important as the memories of being called that he had been taken to the hospital, and other memories of witnessing his mental and physical decline. On the occasion when he had been taken to the hospital because he had three seizures in a row, losing consciousness with each one, I drove to the Fayetteville hospital at seven o'clock at night. I followed the ambulance back to the nursing home when they could find nothing wrong, at three o'clock in the morning. I spent the rest of the night in my car in the staff parking lot, going at five o'clock for coffee to the nearest Hardees, before checking on him in the home. He was sleeping, and I went back to Raleigh to attend an important meeting. I drove back to the Veterans Home that afternoon, had a conference with his nursing home doctor and, exhausted, once again returned home.

Twice more in the following months I was called because of his hospitalization, both times when he developed pneumonia. It was on the second of those emergencies that they diagnosed his inability to swallow even pureed and thickened food or liquid. He was aspirating into his lungs, causing severe pneumonia with high fever and delirium in a matter of hours. Following a swallow-study by the speech pathologist, I was advised that he should not take nourishment by mouth any longer. Having long ago learned from the literature and from the people in my support group who had faced this, I had accepted the fact that I would not allow tube feeding. It would only prolong a life that had no quality and many patients who had stomach tubes were in extreme discomfort. I met with the nursing and nutrition staff at the home, telling them that I knew what stopping nourishment meant, and that I accepted the inevitable turn toward the end. Saying that was much easier than doing it; but his disease process was in control and I could not change it. A feeding tube could not have changed it. He would never be restored to health, physical or mental.

Strangely enough, three days after being released from the hospital, he tried several times to say something to me, appearing stronger and looking at me with recognition.

He would reach for my hand and say, haltingly, "You . . . all. You . . . all." And smile, and squeeze my hand. I was certain in those moments that he knew who I was.

He slipped away quietly in his wheelchair, the fourth day.

★   ★   ★

Michael's journey through Alzheimer's was over, but mine was still following a hard path of memories and feelings. I went back to work after a week, but I could only stay for the morning hours. My fatigue was intense, keeping any sense of peace at bay. When I became tired, I used to describe it as a "sick tired." I would feel the end of my energy coming and have to go home and lie down. The loss of adrenalin meant a total loss of strength. There were times when a feeling of panic took over; split-moments when I realized I hadn't been to Fayetteville lately, and how could I have forgotten to do something so important? Not rational, but real nonetheless. Every time there had been a break in my schedule for the last ten months, I had headed to Fayetteville. Not going was, at first, as painful as going had been.

In those first weeks and even months after his death, I couldn't seem to get beyond the overwhelming sense of what we had been through as we traversed the years of this disease experience. The enormity of it hung over my head like a dark cloud. The cloud was even visible when I closed my eyes, heavy and hovering just above my head.

Slowly, though, I was able to let myself remember our life before Alzheimer's took us on this path through the rocky, fearsome wilderness. Finally, I had a whole picture forming in my head and heart: images and memories of happiness, laughter, wonderful times and troublesome problems. It was a picture of real life, as it happened to real people, in a world that challenged us to live it in the best way we could.

My personal journey through the other side of Alzheimer's will be with me forever. I am, because of it, a different person with a deeper and wider knowledge of life and love. I know that I felt, early on, resentment that disease had precluded our ever resolving the marital problems we had; I felt agonizing pain and wrenching sadness as I watched this vital, intelligent man deteriorate; but now I feel much, much more. Every day, I feel sustaining gratitude for Michael, for our life together in all its comforts and tribulations, and for the faith and love that keeps it all bound in a final blessing.

I gave that rocking chair away, but my last memory of sitting in it by the patio door is of the sweet smell of the next spring and the vivid colors of the flowers; and the birds sang, with a musical message of encouragement.

I had survived living with Alzheimer's and there was, finally, peace in my heart.

A TRIP OF DISCOVERY

Reconnecting with life after Alzheimer's

Fourteen

A Trip of Discovery

In my collection of pictures taken in the summer of 2004, there is a photo of me with Mary Tyler Moore. It's easy to recognize Mary, even in bronze in downtown Minneapolis. She represented to millions of Americans the story of success of a young woman who turned her face and life toward ambition, professionalism and independence, obviously unafraid to create a satisfying and challenging existence with enthusiasm and determination. Having my picture taken standing next to the statue of her tossing her hat in the air was like touching a friend. Thanks to the people of Minneapolis for having the good sense to realize that Minneapolis had become "home" to millions of people because of Mary Tyler Moore and to erect a statue in tribute to her.

The occasion that brought me to Minneapolis started with my son Matt's invitation to visit him at home there. A month earlier, a long-distance conversation had begun between us about this possible trip. The daughter of a friend in Pennsylvania was being married, and Matt kept pressing me to decide whether or not I was going to Pennsylvania to the wedding.

Matt also had an invitation and overcame my hesitation in the end by saying, "If you drive to Pennsylvania, I'll fly down and drive you back to Minneapolis for a visit. You realize, Mom, that you have never been able to visit me anywhere I have lived."

I remember how his words had cut into my heart. It was true. Due to my husband Michael's decline through Alzheimer's disease, I had been no farther away from home than a two-to-three hour drive for seven years. It had been seven months since his death and I was finally beginning to emerge from the fog that had enveloped me while trying to process my feelings about the long illness that had consumed us for so long. It was difficult for me to realize that I could actually go; my job was over for the summer and I wasn't a caregiver at home any more. Now it became difficult to refuse Matt's suggestion. I agreed to meet him in Pennsylvania and go with him, finally, to his home.

After the wedding, when Matt and I were ready to start our two-day road trip to Minneapolis, I was certain that everyone watching and listening could tell I was faking my enthusiasm, an admission I am ashamed to make. In truth, I was reluctant and nervous. It had been so long since Matt and I had spent any time together that was not centered around his stepfather's illness, I could not think of anything we would talk about. We were taking a two-day trip in the same car, and I was devoid of feeling any sense of relevance. I had nothing to contribute to make this trip interesting and couldn't think of any way to make it fun. How could a loving mother feel so uncertain about spending time with her own child? It was unnatural, ungracious, and un . . . well, the self-recriminations went downhill from there. In the days before leaving home, I tried shoring up my sinking feelings by gathering together CDs to listen to in the car. Three of Garrison Keillor's humorous "News from Lake Wobegon" (actually about Minnesota) and three comedy monologues were the only weapons I had against my fear of being a dull companion. After all, I reasoned, even forced laughter would be better than stagnant silence.

It was quite a surprise to discover from the very first mile that my fears and anxieties were all for naught. Matt seemed to be in a true state of pleasure as we drove through places initially new to both of us and other times through places he knew but I had never seen. He talked about having been in these various locations and it was apparent to me that he was sharing years of his life that I had not experienced with him except long-distance. It became a trip of re-connecting, and I gradually recovered the easy relationship we had shared so many years before.

When I asked why we were taking an alternate route as the trip progressed, he grinned and said, "I thought you might like to put your feet in Lake Michigan."

What a thrill! And the next morning when he drove through Chicago because I mentioned never having seen elevated trains, I realized how much we had missed each other and how much of life we still had left to share, and how much fun it was doing it now.

Matt called every friend he had the evening we arrived in Minneapolis, to invite them for hors d'oeuvres the next afternoon.

He said to each of them, "I'm having the come-meet-my-mom-party I told you I was going to have when we got here."

I finally swallowed the lump in my throat but never wiped the grin off my face. His friends came in twos, threes and small groups, bringing with them their familiarity with Matt that I was just beginning to feel once again. The party was a crowded, wonderful experience, full of laughter and comfortable conversation. I realized how grateful I was to be able to know this part of his life now. During his growing-up years, I had always shared his friendships and knowledge of his activities, and it was truly meaningful to feel that closeness again of our parent-and-child relationship. How much I had missed it crowded into my awareness at this opportunity for me to be included once again. I was seeing and coming to know, anew, this now grown child of mine; always loved and cherished, but missed for so long. "Come meet my mom" are words that still echo in my heart as precious.

During the days of sightseeing in that beautiful city, it was obvious that Matt knew it very well and I recognized his pride in this place he now called home. Sharing it with me was one more expression of his caring about my finally visiting him "where he lived."

Going to see the Mary Tyler Moore statue was Matt's idea. Standing there, I felt . . . I truly felt . . . the heaviness of the years of living with illness fade and the joy of living with vibrancy and enthusiasm emerge. Not only did I re-discover my son, but he ushered me into re-discovering myself and living. If I had had a hat, I would have tossed it up in the air.

There is, truly, life after Alzheimer's.

ABOUT THE AUTHOR

Martha-Lee Ellis is the widow of a highly educated man who suffered through ten years of decline due to Alzheimer's disease, writing about how Alzheimer's caused her to change as a result of the progressive changes in him.

She graduated Magna Cum Laude with a Bachelor of Arts in psychology, holds a Masters degree in education and completed post-graduate work in counseling for families of persons with disabilities. She served as visiting instructor in the field of special education and program administration for two North Carolina universities. She is an experienced speaker, lecturer, nonprofit program administrator, and consultant in the field of disabilities.

During a thirty-year career as Executive Director of a non-profit school for children with disabilities, she was a volunteer advocate for programs serving children with disabilities for members of the North Carolina General Assembly.

She currently serves on the Board of Directors of the Frankie Lemmon Foundation for children with disabilities, the Meredith College Social Work Advisory Board, and the Board of Directors of the Ruth Sheets Adult Care Center, all in Raleigh, NC.

She continues active participation in the support group sponsored by the Ruth Sheets Adult Care Center for families and caregivers of older persons with dementia and other conditions of frailty.

CPSIA information can be obtained at www.ICGtesting.com
Printed in the USA
BVOW060929150312

285182BV00002B/3/P